My Parent's Keeper:

Adult Children of the Emotionally Disturbed

Eva Marian Brown, M.S.W.

Edited by Nina Sonenberg

"When I think about my childhood, I always think, 'Highway robbery!' I just feel robbed. I feel strongly that no child should ever go through that."

-An ACMI

"I still feel really sad at what happened to both of us. She should never have been left alone to take care of me. She should never have been left alone at all. We were both victims."

-An ACMI's mother

Table of Contents

Acknowledgments

I wish to express my indebtedness to those many colleagues whose writings about Adult Children of Alcoholics issues have opened the door to an expanded exploration of dysfunctional families. Among those whose work have influenced me are Claudia Black, Sharon Wegscheider-Cruse, John Bradshaw, Anne Wilson Schaef, Stephanie Brown, and Tim Cermak. A special thanks to Alice Miller, who has written about complex developmental issues with a warmth and accessibility that make her books of value not only to the professional but to our clients as well.

Many people have contributed to making my experience of writing this book an enjoyable one. I first want to thank all my friends and colleagues whose faith in me and enthusiasm about this project have helped me keep a steady course toward accomplishing my goals. Among these, special thanks to Eli Leon, Andrea Lappen, Gordon Holleb, Jay Earley, Nancy Friedman, and Suzanne Slyman. In addition, I want to express my gratitude to Steven Goldbart, whose warmth, clarity, and optimism have greatly expanded my sense of what is possible. A special thanks to David Widelock for his consistent support and intelligent involvement in this work.

I want to acknowledge the many clients whose courage in facing and dealing with their difficult histories have inspired this project. I'm indebted to those individuals who, by volunteering to be interviewed, contributed greatly to the richness of the book.

I'd like to express my appreciation to Matthew McKay, for his gentle and constructive guidance in the writing process. My thanks also to Nina Sonenberg, for her careful and thoughtful editing, and to Anne Irving, for transcribing many hours of tape with an attention and interest that went far beyond the job description.

Preface

This book is written for and about the many people who grew up with parents with severe emotional problems. Throughout the book, I use the term "ACMI"–Adult Children of the Mentally Ill. This term refers to adults who grew up with a parent suffering from a serious psychological impairment that profoundly affected the functioning of both the parent and the family. Some ACMIs had a parent who was diagnosed and treated for a mental illness such as schizophrenia or manic-depression. Others had a parent whose disturbance was not tended to, but who was violent or erratic in his or her behavior, or who showed symptoms of severe depression or anxiety. While ACMIs share many problems with other children of dysfunctional parents, such as Adult Children of Alcoholics, they also have had a set of experiences which is unique to them as a group.

In selecting the acronym "ACMI" for the adult survivors of troubled parents, I chose the term "mentally ill" rather than the more general (and sometimes euphemistic) term, "emotionally disturbed." In doing so, I want to challenge the stigma associated with mental illness by helping to put the term into more common and open usage. I also would like to encourage a shift in our perception of mental illness. Instead of approaching it as a strange and scary phenomenon, I wish to help bring it into the more manageable and even hopeful realm of treatable disease. Just as alcoholism has recently come out of the closet, mental illness, which touches millions of families, needs to become an openly addressed fact of life.*

The book is organized in such a way that the initial chapters will give you a description of the background and problems confronting the ACMI. The later chapters will talk about ways of overcoming the problems many ACMIs face as adults.

It is my hope that ACMIs will find this book a source of support and encouragement when dealing with the inevitable wounds resulting from growing up in a dysfunctional family. My intent is to provide you with some tools for tackling your issues on your own. I don't, however, intend to imply that deep-seated hurts can in all instances be satisfactorily healed with these methods. While this book will help you identify some important themes in your life, some of you will find that you want or need some professional guidance. A dialogue with a therapist can offer support for a deeper exploration and understanding of your history, emotions, and current behavior.

The quotations in this book are taken from the transcripts of many hours of interviews with ACMIs. The ACMIs whom I interviewed generously shared the details of their experiences in the hopes of helping other people who grew up in similar circumstances.

Eva Marian Brown
Oakland, California
May, 1989

*The subtitle of this book was changed from "Adult Children of the Mentally Ill" to "Adult Children of the Emotionally Disturbed" on the advice of the book distributors, who felt they'd be unable to present it to the bookstores with the original title. Apparently the term "mental illness" would only be well received in a title intended for mental health professionals. This is an example of how mental illness is viewed as a problem discussed only by the professionals who treat it, not by those whose lives it affects.

Part I

Early Hurts
and Old Wounds

"I always wanted to leave my past behind, not think about it and just move on with my life. But I found that so much of me was trapped in the past, in the pain and patterns of my childhood, that I came to realize that I couldn't really move forward until I understood my history and came to terms with it."

–An ACMI

1

Parentified Children

"Allowing myself to be a child, learning how to be one–since I wasn't a child for very long–knowing that it's okay is real hard for me. Sometimes when I catch myself being carefree, I feel bad about it. I feel, well, I'm an adult, so I'm supposed to be responsible."

People who were raised by a mentally ill parent often share a similar set of feelings and behaviors. These similarities grow out of spending one's childhood trying to cope with a disturbed parent. Life in a dysfunctional family of this sort often encourages a child to enter into a role reversal with his or her disturbed parent. The child will frequently become a little parent, worrying about the needs and limitations of the adults. Since their own wishes for care and guidance cannot be met, such children tend to bury their needs in order to take on this caretaker role. The result is a "parentified child." In adulthood, having been forced to grow up much too soon, parentified children continue to pay a high price.

As adults, many parentified children have a very hard time with intimacy. As one ACMI (Adult Child of the Mentally Ill) attests:

> "Boy, it's real hard being dependent. I take so much control in relationships. I won't allow myself to rely on anyone–I have to take *all* the responsibility. To let someone hold me is hard. I feel like I'm reverting back to being a child, getting the things that I didn't get when I was younger. I can let myself have it for a while, and then I start saying: 'No, you can't. You have to stand on your own two feet. You have to take care of yourself. You *can't* rely on anyone else.' And I get these real alone moods, and I can't be touched."

A Frightening Childhood

You may not remember all of what it was like to be a small child in your family, but you probably can recall enough of your early family life to determine whether you were a parentified child.

Picture yourself at age two, toddling around. At that age, you need an environment in which you can explore new objects and try out new behaviors with people. You also need a caretaker who will stop you from falling down the cellar steps or will let you know in no uncertain terms that kicking people in the shins is not okay.

If you grew up with a disturbed parent, you may have found–to use the simplest example–that you lacked a parent who would prevent you from falling down the steps. Perhaps your parent wouldn't stop you, in a constructive way, from hurting people around you when you were having a tantrum. You may have had a parent who, when you hit him or her, hauled off and hit you back. Or perhaps your parent took a two-year-old's frustrated fit as a personal affront and burst into tears, asking you, "Why do you hate me so much?" Or you may have had a parent who didn't respond to you at all, who didn't seem to notice what you were going through, or who didn't reflect it back to you in a way that showed you that he or she understood your needs.

Typically, a child with an emotionally disturbed parent finds the natural dependency of childhood to be a frightening experience. There you are, looking to the adults around you for guidance and safety in order to grow and flourish. You need your parents to provide you with enough physical and emotional room to explore the world. Just as important, you need your parents to say no and to establish limits when you are putting yourself in danger. These very simple functions are provided appropriately at every stage of a child's development when parents are functioning adequately.

Most children have imperfect parenting. No human being is perfect, and therefore no parents are perfect. And no child needs perfect parents. In psychology there's a phrase, "the good-enough mother." What you needed when you were a child was a good-enough parent, a parent who provided a good-enough set of responses so that you developed a sense of yourself and a sense of being safe in the world.

Picture yourself as a small child not being able to count on an appropriate response from your parent. Maybe your mother stays in bed all day, depressed and withdrawn. She simply isn't there for you emotionally. Think how scary that might have been. Or imagine that your father swings wildly between showering you with affection and bursting into sudden rages. You feel frightened and confused because his emotions have little to do with your behavior. As one ACMI put it:

"There was a way she always seemed mean and at the same time really fragile. She always felt fragile. I always ended up feeling like I was taking care of her because she would change her moods so easily."

Another ACMI talks about his father, whose anger was physically out of control:

"I can remember hiding, finding a door that could be locked because I was so afraid of his temper and his power and his strength. He would frequently attack me verbally, too."

As a child you respond to this absence of good parenting with a lot of fear. Your environment feels chaotic. There's no safety, no predictability. There's no one minding the store while you do the necessary childhood exploring of your environment. This fear is also mixed with feelings of anger and loss.

Often these feelings conflict. For example, as a child you may have concluded that you weren't getting what you needed because you were undeserving. At the same time, in a secret corner of your mind, you may have harbored a fierce feeling that you had every right to get your needs met.

Another feeling you may have had as a child was powerlessness. You couldn't do anything to get your needs met. At the same time, you may have felt responsible for things that were actually outside of your control. For example, you may have at one and the same time believed that you were powerless to make Mommy love you and yet so powerful that you had caused her to become ill.

As you grow older, your environment expands but the predominant feeling of fear remains. You go off to school and there isn't a safe nest to come home to. The new events of your expanding world become frightening instead of exciting because there's no one to guide you, comfort you, or set appropriate limits.

Some of you came home to a withdrawn parent:

"She was just real quiet. She slept a lot. She took a lot of Valiums. I remember her constantly taking these pills. And I remember she stayed up at night a lot of times, walking around the house. She was really withdrawn, really nervous. She didn't take care of herself. And she didn't take care of the house. It was pretty chaotic inside of our house, to say the least."

Others of you faced an angry caretaker:

"Some very vivid memories I have are of her being very angry, being agitated very easily, yelling and screaming, having fights with my father, and just being in a rage a lot. And I remember her pretty clearly one summer. I was about six at the time. We rented a house on the beach and I remember her saying things like, 'I'm having a nervous breakdown.' I felt very trapped and scared. I mean, there wasn't a lot I could do."

So what do you do to avoid simply sitting in a corner shaking with fear? How do you go on in a world that is frightening, that seems to lack the necessary safety net of childhood?

Control Replaces Feeling

Most of you attempt to provide the safety for yourselves. Since you can see that your parents don't have the necessary control, you have to get into the driver's seat. There is no other solution if you're to continue to grow, develop, and move on with your life. But providing the support for yourself at such a young age and in the face of so much fear can only be accomplished at a cost. What you sacrifice is the right to feel and express the whole range of human emotion: fear, anger, even love. You learn to control your feelings.

Three ACMIs from quite different backgrounds describe a similar process of learning to feel as little as possible:

> "I remember being really numb. It was the feeling of just being a vegetable, of feeling as numb as possible."

*

> "I think I cut off from my feelings a lot and focused on getting done what I had to get done, which was taking care of her and listening. A lot of the night I would listen. I would sleep with one ear pricked to hear if she'd fall down, which she did frequently in the middle of the night. She'd get up to go to the bathroom and fall down, and then I'd have to go down the stairs and help her."

*

> "Well, I think my father is very afraid of emotion. So that probably would have been the way the house was, even if she hadn't had those problems. Everything was so shut down emotionally that everybody was just dead—emotionally dead. There were no real

fights; there was not much laughing or joy either. There was just this middle zone of nothingness."

In a dysfunctional family, you quickly discover that your feelings are a source of danger. You provide safety for yourself by clamping down on your emotions. For example, if you get angry, your anger, rather than being met with a firm but gentle control, is met with the enormous force of an adult's rage, or with a disproportionate amount of fear or hurt from your parent. Or perhaps your anger is simply allowed to run out of control and escalate to a point where it's destructive and scary for you.

So you learn to control yourself. You squelch your anger and your sadness and your fear. Since the response is anything but comforting when you turn to one of your parents in tears looking for comfort, you begin to avoid the rebuffs by *not* turning to them. If your feelings seem too much for your parent to handle, you avoid your feelings. When you see that the parent you're approaching is feeling even more fear and confusion than you are, you begin to realize that you will have to be the one in charge.

As one ACMI says:

"I felt like a mother minding her child. I really felt that way. I had to know, every minute, where she was. Even when she was in her bedroom, I'd walk by and stand outside the door, listening to see if I heard anything. Or sometimes I'd even go in—you know, just pop in and say hello. And I would never say to her, 'Well, I was just checking on you to make sure you're breathing,' but that's what I was doing. It was like a family who worries about a child who's been sick, or had a child who died of sudden crib death."

Over the years, as you repeatedly experience your parent's inadequacy in responding to your feelings, and as you witness their own internal chaos, you build a life around being in control. Being in control becomes the most important thing in your life; your survival depends upon it. The world around you, your home, is a scary, unpredictable place. The grown-ups who should ideally be providing you with a measure of safety are not a source of safety and strength for you. Therefore you push away any feelings that might interfere with a stoic sense of surviving at any cost.

Caring for the Caretaker

A further development occurs for many of you because, like all children, you're attached to your parents–but the closeness between you takes an unusual turn. As you gain control over your feelings, you attempt to take control of your parent's chaos as well. In other words, you try to take care of your disturbed parent. This caretaking, while it may at times look and even feel like loving concern, has another purpose. It's largely motivated by the desire to help and heal your caretaker so that he or she will be able to take care of *you*. Your instinct, usually not put into words, goes like this: "If I can only make Mommy feel better, then she'll be here for me; she'll be able to take better care of me."

This caretaking takes many forms. With a depressed parent, you may do your best to cheer him or her up, bringing smiles and reassurance. With an angry parent, you learn ways of sidestepping his or her anger, being careful not to trigger it. You learn how to defuse it. With a highly anxious parent, you are the one who calms and reassures. With a parent who is out of contact with the concrete aspects of reality, you may end up cooking, cleaning, shopping, or providing physical care. In any case, you take on his or her problem as your own. You hope that if only you can *give* enough support, maybe you will finally *get* some.

Here a number of ACMIs talk about strategies they adopted in attempting to meet their disturbed mother's needs:

> "I felt like I had to reassure her that everything was okay, that she wasn't a bad person, just try to calm her down. I felt like I had to act in ways that wouldn't upset her or agitate her more. I just tried to be a good girl and not cause her to get more upset."

*

> "I don't think I've ever gotten as low as I remember her looking. I was worried about her, because I didn't know what she was going to do. I really was afraid that she was suicidal. I'm pretty sure she was. I know she would try different things, although I don't think she really wanted to die. I found myself going through the house, wondering, kind of checking, seeing where she was. I always needed to know where she was, that she was okay. If she was outside, I would look out and see where she was out in the yard, working."

*

> "I was like my mother's best friend. I was hardly ever out of her sight when she was home. I remember spending all my time with her. I was the perfect little good girl. I got straight A's. I did all my chores. It

was never enough. I was still bad, but I tried to be perfect."

*

"Looking back on it now, it was terrifying. I think I just held myself together and focused on taking care of her, as best I could. That meant putting her to bed every night–she really resisted going to sleep. And she smoked, and so I would always be pleading with her to put out the cigarettes. I never slept very well because I'd be listening. For some reason she was downstairs and I was upstairs. And it was this big house, and it was way out in the middle of the woods and there were lots of sounds all around. I would be scared of robbers and foxes and things that kids are scared of, but there wasn't anyone to call on for help or comfort. I could scream at the top of my lungs and she wouldn't get up. So I think I lived with a lot of terror that I just kind of pushed down."

*

"I almost felt like on some level I had to take care of her. She seemed like a real drag; she just didn't have a lot of energy. I felt very alone, because I didn't have anyone to play with. She wasn't playing with me, and in fact was just saying things that I couldn't really deal with. I spent time trying to reassure her that things were okay. It just seems bizarre that a four- or five-year-old had to do that."

*

"A bunch of times that year my mother tried to kill herself. One time she jumped in the river in the middle of the winter. A neighbor brought her back at two in the morning, and just sort of shoved her into my arms. I didn't know what the medical treatment was–I mean, put her in a cold bath and then heat it up more? I really wanted to ask the neighbor to stay and help but he was this man and he wasn't supposed to see her naked. So there were neighbors involved; the neighbors on both sides knew. In fact, one of the neighbors at one point kept her pills for her and kind of doled them out every day. But I didn't really get emotional support from them."

*

"I can't describe how it happened, you know. It all just happened. It was so subtle. Nobody said, 'Well, you're going to take this role in the family.' It just happened. For some reason I felt a lot of responsibility to help hold the family together, at the real exclusion of being a pre-teenager, a burgeoning, budding adolescent. That absolutely went by the wayside. It just disappeared, all those years."

The Damage to Your Self-Esteem

One of the problems that most of you encounter with these caretaking efforts is the hopelessness of the task. In most instances, your efforts to heal your parent are destined not to work. There's no way you can actually repair the severe damage your parent's psyche has already suffered. Of course, as a child you can't know that this job is too large for you. You may therefore pin your sense of adequacy on achieving this goal. You become invested in this task not only to heal your parent but also as a measure of your own abilities. You think, "When I can make mommy smile, I feel happy, and I feel like a good girl." Slowly but surely your self-esteem becomes entwined with your success or failure in restoring your parent to more adequate functioning. The sad truth is that most of you are fated to fail in your task. And as you do, your self-esteem becomes more and more eroded.

At this point you have three basic problems. You feel unsafe in the world because your family hasn't taught you the necessary interpersonal skills. You have a deep feeling of aloneness and deprivation because your parent isn't providing reliable and loving contact. And you feel terrible about yourself because you consider it your fault that you aren't being adequately taken care of. In the midst of this massive struggle there is little room to be a playful, light-hearted child. The result is a typical profile of the parentified child—serious, responsible, intense, unusually sensitive, and often readily hurt.

At some point in your life, perhaps in your teen years, some of you get sick of this good-child role. You rebel and become a troublemaker. You attempt to throw off the yoke of premature responsibility. You begin to raise enough hell so that people finally have to pay attention to you.

Most of you, however, take a different path. You move into adulthood with a keen sensitivity to others' pain and a tendency to rescue and take care of people who are close to you. You also find it difficult to accept caretaking when it's offered. Because you interpret your lack of adequate parenting as a negative statement about your self-worth, you don't feel that you are deserving. You fear that while you *appear* responsible and loving, if you really let someone get close, they'll discover the bad you, the inadequate you deep inside.

This buried feeling of not being okay makes it very hard for many of you to allow intimate relationships to develop. Being close involves letting another person really know who you are. This kind of authentic contact is very frightening to you if you have serious doubts about your worthiness.

Many ACMIs aren't aware that this lack of self-esteem is one of the major reasons they are unable to get close to people. You might know that something is lacking and that you have difficulties either forming or maintaining really intimate relationships, but you might not know why. Knowing that it's the frightened child within you that you're protecting is an important step toward learning to reach out to others, and toward allowing yourself to be the care-receiver as well as the care-taker in a relationship.

2

Survivor's Guilt: The Price of Leaving Home

"I remember feeling really guilty about going away to college, even though I went just fifty miles away. I went home several times a year. Some of the time my mother would be sort of okay and some of the time she would be really sick. She continued to be in and out of institutions from then until now. I felt guilty a lot of the time–being away, and trying to go on with my life. I felt somehow that I shouldn't be enjoying myself if she was so miserable."

ACMIs often harbor an enormous sense of guilt and inadequacy. Many ACMIs struggle with these feelings throughout childhood. The burden of guilt often reaches a crisis point around the issue of leaving home.

In a healthy family, the process of growing up and moving toward independence takes place gradually and smoothly. If you grow up in a well-functioning family, by the time you reach your late teens you have been given many of the necessary tools for building a satisfying adult life. With the backing and the blessing of your family, you take that enormous step away from home to explore a lifestyle of your own choosing.

The Pain of Saying Goodbye

The ACMI arrives at adulthood lacking some necessary skills and without supportive parents in the background. These years can be confusing and painful. An ACMI about to leave home must face abandoning a task undertaken many years earlier: healing the emotional wounds of a mentally ill parent. Of course, the task was always an impossible one, but as a child you didn't know that. This is one source of the enormous burden of grief and guilt you carry with you as you try to move away from your family.

For a number of you, leaving behind a disturbed parent whose pain you cannot assuage isn't the only goodbye you face. Some of you are also leaving a healthier parent who must now take on more of the burden of caring for your ill parent. Quite a few of you are also saying goodbye to younger siblings toward whom you have felt protective and, in some cases, for whom you have functioned as a surrogate parent.

Chapter 1 describes how the ACMI becomes a caretaker, tending to the needs of everyone around. Chances are that in your family you often took on that role. Even those of you who didn't become the family caretaker report that it was painful to leave home. You witnessed the family members who were staying behind struggling with, and sometimes seemingly drowning in, the chaos of your family. Many of you say these were the most difficult years of your life, as you were emotionally pulled back and forth between your concern for your family members and your yearning to leave.

For many of you, each positive step toward establishing a life of your own is accompanied by a nagging feeling of wrongdoing. You may ask yourself: "Is it okay to abandon all those people who are in pain? Is it okay to try to make a healthy, happy, satisfying life for myself when people I love are suffering so much? Is it okay to give up on the task of helping them in order to build for myself a life that feels worth living?" Here an ACMI describes how it felt to go away to college:

> "I think I felt fear and some guilt about leaving home. I remember the day I left for college. My father picked me up and I looked up at the window where my mother was standing. She was sobbing, and I thought: 'This is it.' It hit me that I was probably never going to live with her again. I think I did feel some guilt, like 'Oh, my God, is she going to be able to survive? Is she going to be able to make it?' And when I got to school, I became really depressed."

Another ACMI talks about using geographical distance as a way to separate:

> "I think one of the things that saved me was getting far away from home. I went a thousand miles or so away to college, not really intentionally but it sort of happened. Looking back, I could have chosen another school that was closer, but *no way.* I dropped out of school after a year and moved *three* thousand miles away. It wasn't entirely conscious, but I think for me it was a way to save myself. I had to have a physical distance because there was no way I could get any emotional distance at first. I had to just get out of there."

Separation Strategies

The specifics of how ACMIs work out this separation problem differ widely. Some of you fled your chaotic homes very early in your lives, instinctively understanding that getting out was the only way to survive. You may have run away from home or married very early or found a willing relative with whom to live. Some of you found that the only way to leave home was to break off contact altogether. Others found yourselves staying at home far too long, tending to the needs of your family way beyond an age where it made sense, and denying your need to build a separate life. And a lot of you have run back and forth between your own life and the life of your family. You've attempted to build a new life, perhaps with a new family, yet you still tend to the constant needs and crises of your old family. You are pushed and pulled between two worlds.

A few of you have made some peace with saying goodbye to the family of your childhood. You remain in as much contact as makes sense to you and don't allow your present life to become too disrupted by the ever changing conditions in your old family. But most of you feel that in one way or another you have had to psychologically amputate parts of yourself in order to survive. You may have cut off some of your feelings for your mother or your father or your siblings. You may have given up some of what you wanted as an adult, cutting into your own needs in order to continue to offer support to your family.

This juggling act is never quite finished. With the passage of time, your parents grow old. Along with the problems of aging parents that everybody encounters, your problems are multiplied by the fact that one of your parents never was able to function well. Often that parent needs caretaking more than ever, as physical infirmity adds extra stress to his or her emotional disability. With these changes in your family's situation, your sense of conflict may grow. And your guilt at continuing on with your own life may become overwhelming. The next section will help you recognize the signs of conscious or unconscious guilt.

The Price of Guilt

When you are having difficulty completing a healthy separation from your family, one symptom, without you realizing it, may be that you behave in ways that are self-punishing. You unconsciously say to yourself, "Because I abandoned my family in their pain, I don't deserve to have a successful and enjoyable life." For example, you may find that you deprive yourself of success and achievements. Perhaps you don't allow yourself meaningful work or other productive activities. Or perhaps whenever you begin to achieve, you sabotage that achievement by creating unnecessary failures. Or you settle for a level of achievement far below your capabilities.

For example, you may decide to learn a new skill and find that you are quite talented at it. Inexplicably you stop putting the necessary effort into the new project. Or you may do well at your job until others begin to notice that you are competent. Then you slack off or in other ways avoid the acknowledgment that would come to you if you persevered. There are numerous ways of making sure that you never become too good at what you are doing, thus guaranteeing that you never enjoy the praise of others.

or don't allow self pride in achievement —
+ supreme guilt in advance + after big worry

Another sign that you may be operating from a guilt feeling appears when you consistently avoid pleasurable experiences. Perhaps you deprive yourself of enjoyable contact with other people. Maybe you don't permit yourself to have playful activities. Perhaps the only activity in which you feel comfortable is one that's goal-oriented and productive. ACMIs are often stoic and hard-working, responsible and serious.

There can be a number of reasons for these traits, but the feelings of guilt about your achievements and pleasures in life often have a lot to do with why you can't allow yourself rich and satisfying work and play.

Another symptom of your sense of guilt arises in relationships. You may find that you feel compelled to fix any problem that a friend may have. Giving support and empathy is never enough. You become very uncomfortable if you can't be the actual problem-solver. This fix-it compulsion is an indirect way of expressing your discomfort at being unable to solve the problems in your family. A friend's dilemma stirs up those old helpless feelings about your family situation.

Working through survivor's guilt tends to be a long process. So much of your self-limiting and self-punishing behavior is habitual and unconscious. But as you begin to examine different areas of your life, you'll get better at spotting those times when you feel compelled to atone for the pain of the people you grew up with. Each time you can challenge the guilt you feel and allow yourself a little more pleasure, you're moving toward a healthy independence from your dysfunctional family.

3

Crazy Minnie's Daughter Mary–Like Mother, Like Child?

"I always felt that other people thought they were better than our family. They just had that attitude. I don't really know how I sensed that, how I got that impression, but I definitely did."

Many of you find that as you take the necessary steps away from your family and work to build a life of your own it's not really possible to leave your past behind. For example, holidays and social functions often remain entwined with your family, whether you choose it that way or not. For many of you, there are still people in your life who knew you when you were growing up. You may even maintain close contact with some of your relatives. And the world about us continues to view each of us as part of a whole, as a person with roots in a family. You probably have friends who are curious about your roots and ask about your family.

A Family That Isn't "Normal"

As you move through the different phases of your life, there are times when it's obvious that your family is considered peculiar. Here an ACMI describes her adolescence:

> "When I was still fairly young, I can remember always being embarrassed about my mother. She hadn't been declared emotionally ill yet, but she always used to yell at the neighborhood kids, and she threw rocks at pigeons. She was one of those people who always said the wrong thing socially. My sister and I used to just *die*. Especially when you're that age, part of you is really cackling and chuckling and saying, ' Ha-ha-ha, isn't that funny,' but part of you is *dying,* wondering, 'How could this be my mother?'"

Many of you grew up in families where there were other relatives around, at least part of the time. In some cases, these relatives–aunts, uncles, grandparents, cousins–provided some modeling and some of the support of healthier families. Some of you, however, as you became more aware of your relatives' attitudes toward your distressed family, discovered that you were being viewed in negative ways. Perhaps you sensed that you were being pitied. While you might have enjoyed some sympathy, the pity didn't feel good at all. Or maybe adults around you avoided talking about your parent's illness. As one ACMI recalls:

> "I think they were trying to protect us kids in some ways. But I don't think they talked about it among themselves either. I think they just didn't know how

to deal with it. They couldn't understand why my mom was like that."

A few of your relatives may have acted wary of the disturbed parent in your family. They may even have been suspicious of *you*—watching you, wondering whether you would turn out "normal." If your disturbed parent deteriorated over the years, as is often the case, relatives may have pulled back more and more from a difficult and perhaps frightening situation.

An ACMI describes the mixture of isolation and shame she felt when she was left to care for her mother alone:

> "I didn't have anyone to come home to. When she would be in the hospital and I was in school, I would come home to an empty house and end up going out to County Hospital to visit her. This was after my father's death. It seemed like it was a subject that wasn't okay to talk about. People looked at you like *you* were crazy, like there was something totally wrong with your whole family. It's a reflection on you."

Sometimes even in the hospital setting, the sense of stigma and isolation continued:

> "If you get into the elevator at the hospital and get off on the psych ward, people look at you in a different way. It's as if there's something sicker about people there than somewhere else in the hospital. And that's just stuff that society sticks us with. That's not real. They're not untouchable people. They're not diseased. People often don't even visit the people upstairs. They do if they have any other ill-

ness, but they don't visit them *there;* they somehow don't think they need the caring and loving."

Adulthood and the Extended Family

Some of you have talked about stresses in trying to stay connected with your relatives once you reached adulthood. You feel that there is a stigma attached to you. They know you as Crazy Minnie's daughter Mary, and it feels as if you're being watched carefully for signs that perhaps you, too, will turn out to have a mental illness.

Sometimes your siblings try to divorce themselves from any association with their disturbed parent, hoping to avoid this pain and stigma:

> "The more I deal with my mother's illness, the more pervasive it seems to me. And I want to be able to talk to my sister about it. The hard part about it now is that no one else in my family wants to talk about it. My older sister is the one that took care of me when I was little. She's really the only person in my family I'm close to right now, and she hates talking about it. As soon as I start in on something, she tries to change the subject as fast as she can. She doesn't really want to think about how it affected her."

Being included in family events—weddings, holidays, celebrations of any kind—may be a rarity. When you *are* included, you may be received coolly. Your left wondering whether you're being shunned, or whether you're simply being "paranoid." These subtle and sometimes not-so-subtle rejections extend their effect beyond your dealings with your family. They make you even more wary of sharing your background with newfound friends and partners. You find yourself wondering whether people who grew up in families that function better than yours can really understand your background.

The ACMI With Strangers and Friends

Do new people in your life look at you differently when they learn of mental illness in your family? Are friends able to tolerate your natural ups and downs, your moods, and your emotions without being alarmed that perhaps you're going off the deep end? These are questions many ACMIs wrestle with.

You already learned in your family that expressing your needs and feelings tended to get you into trouble and leave you frustrated and unsatisfied. In your adult life, as you begin to test out whether you can be freer to express yourself, you worry that people's responses to you might be colored by their knowledge of your background. One of the statements ACMIs repeat in group therapy sessions is what a relief it is to be in a roomful of other people who grew up with an emotionally disturbed parent. This is partly because the people in the room don't assume that since your mother or father was disturbed, *you* must be emotionally disabled.

Rites of Passage

There are many occasions in your adult life when there is a coming together of the past and the present. This often happens during transitions from one part of your life to another: graduation from high school or from college, for instance, and major events like weddings and births. These are events where your friends and acquaintances gather together with your family members. Many of you face painful dilemmas over whether to invite a mentally ill parent to attend a ceremony, or how to explain the absence of one or both of your parents. Even holidays and birthdays can be problematic. One ACMI describes being the class valedictorian:

> "I was on the stage and I was giving my speech. I looked around and I saw my mom. In a way, I wished she wasn't there. It was pretty embarrassing to have her there, but I couldn't stand not having her there either. It was a real double-bind."

These situations are difficult no matter how much you grow and strengthen yourself. They are made more difficult by unresolved conflicts about your past. Each Mother's Day or Father's Day may stir you up anew, not only practically (should you acknowledge the occasion?) but also emotionally (what is the event supposed to mean, what does it actually evoke for you in your feelings and memories?).

Your Aging Parents

Your Parents as Grandparents

Some of you are now married and have children. You yearn to provide your children with doting grandparents. At the same time, you want to protect your child from some of the frightening or painful aspects of being in close contact with the parent who was so difficult for *you* to handle as a child. Some of you are deeply disappointed at being unable to see your children enjoy a relaxed and loving grandparent/

grandchild relationship, a double disappointment because it reminds you again of your own robbed childhood. You may also regret having to limit or deny your parents the pleasures of being grandparents. This source of nourishment and meaning in old age may largely be lost for your disturbed parent.

Facing Your Parents' Physical Decline

You will eventually face the difficult mid-life issue of your parents growing old. This is a situation most adult children have to come to grips with at some point. But for you as an ACMI it involves the increasing need and dependence of a parent who *always* had some difficulty managing his or her own life. This increasing dependence reactivates all the old conflict in you about taking care of your parent's needs instead of taking care of your own. For many of you, this phase of your adult life evokes an enormous increase in your feelings of ambivalence and guilt. At times it may produce a setback in the progress you've made in learning to take care of yourself.

Over the years, some of you have been buffered by a more functional parent who managed the needs of your emotionally distressed parent. As the emotionally healthier parent ages, facing declining strength and other physical difficulties, you may increasingly feel pressured to step in and take care of both of them.

"When you've dealt your whole life with one parent being really depressed and the other one being really strong, somehow always keeping it together and taking care of the sick one (at least, when she wasn't institutionalized), and then the 'well' parent starts to get really sick, not only physically but showing mental signs of things happening.... I think I first realized my dad was having difficulty from his letters. I just thought: I'm not going to worry about it; this must be the normal aging process. I haven't been really close to other people who've gotten into their mid-seventies. And I didn't think about it too much, at least for a while, until the automobile accident and then the diagnosis that my dad had Parkinson's disease."

Facing Your Family History

These family crises often cause emotional upheavals for the ACMI, upsetting the stability you've worked so hard to create. As an ACMI, you may have been forced to re-examine yourself and your relationship to your family. The majority of you, at some point in your lives, feel the need to look at your background, to explore the forces that shaped you into the person you are today.

To the degree that you've dealt with issues and feelings about your childhood and have been able to build nurturing and satisfying adult relationships, you'll bring to these crises more inner strength, as well as a network of supportive friends you can turn to when these problems arise.

For those of you who are having difficulty in being close to other people and allowing yourself to be nurtured and supported, these family problems may be overwhelmingly stressful. The first step toward getting more support involves taking the risk of sharing more of your history and your feelings with close friends and perhaps with a supportive therapist or in a safe group setting.

You may be reluctant to admit to yourself that you need support to get through these family crises. You're used to toughing it out, denying how much your family still affects your present life. And up to now, your survival may have seemed to depend on such a stoic, stiff upper-lip attitude. You might have been telling yourself, "My past is my past and I can leave it all behind." But this stance doesn't work in the long run.

"I learned how to be really strong–I can get through anything. And I don't think I realized the toll that so-called strength took on me. There *was* actual strength there, but some of it was really clenching your whole body, your fists and everything else, and just going through it. I had to give up a lot to do it, a lot of myself. So under all that strength was a lot of terror that I didn't have any time to feel. It was a way to survive, but it wasn't true strength."

Most of you find it an enormous relief to let go of the denial and stoicism that colored your life. Since the majority of you are survivors, you will find that you have a number of excellent coping skills. You also have an inner strength to draw on as you open up some of the painful memories and issues of your childhood. It is not an easy journey. It is one that requires a great deal of support from friends and, for some, a therapeutic setting. However, as you begin to reclaim and understand feelings that you buried long ago, you can begin to deal more effectively with family crises, as well as all the other tough spots life will confront you with. As you start to understand the connections between your past and present, the fabric of your life may begin to seem more whole.

4

Emotions and Control–Learning To Allow Intimacy

"I learned how to appease. And, for the most part, I *could* appease my mother, but it was at the price of my spirit. When I didn't, she would fly into rages. She would also go into silence for long periods of time. They were very angry silences, silences filled with blame."

As a child, you developed certain ways of coping with an ill parent who couldn't provide the support you needed to fully explore yourself and the world around you. These coping strategies enabled you to survive your childhood, but they became counterproductive once you left home. Most of you find that you have the same style of interacting with people now that you used in your family. The problems that arise in your current relationships originate in your continuing use of these old strategies in brand-new situations.

"Whatever feeble attempts I made in the teenage years to develop relationships, even within my family, didn't succeed. So, I grew up not understanding in any way how satisfying relationships can be and how you could develop good relationships with people. I didn't know you could have an intimate relationship with somebody and get angry with them, and they'd still love you. I never had a concept of that when I was growing up. I was trying to be good and not rock the boat, because there were enough problems as it was. I was trying to be so perfect... and you know, that's been haunting me ever since."

To some degree, everybody brings old learning into each new experience, but the hallmark of the ACMI is a certain rigidity in one's approach to new situations. Most of you grew up with a lot of fear. You responded to that fear by clamping down on the wide range of emotions you otherwise would have experienced under safer circumstances. You were left with a heightened sensitivity to others' needs and feelings and with a tendency to be out of touch with your own emotions. As a child you learned to get along by being aware of the feelings of the people in your environment. As an adult you continue to get along with others by noticing what they need and attempting to provide it for them. This sensitivity to others, a very beautiful quality, becomes a liability when your own needs are excluded.

Typical ACMI Relationships

"In the past, I've gotten involved with people who might not blatantly need caretaking, but who really couldn't give me a lot of attention. Usually they came from really abused, deprived backgrounds. I always felt that their life was so much worse than mine, you could just never love that person enough. So I would get really focused on them. One person was a pothead. Another was an alcoholic. Another woman had been terribly abused. I found people who really needed a lot of care. That way I could avoid my own needs, because the other person just seemed so much needier than me. I've really had to do a lot of therapy and work hard to get out of that. I'm now in a relationship that doesn't have those elements. I'm not saying I'm all better, but I've managed to get out of that pattern."

One way to understand your internal conflicts about relationships is to look at the kinds of partners you choose. If you're like many ACMIs, you'll find that you limit yourself to one of three types of relationships.

The ACMI as Caretaker

You may choose to be with somebody who needs and demands a lot of caretaking. With this individual you continue the emotional role you performed for your disturbed parent.

One ACMI describes her first marriage:

"I think what attracted me to him was that I felt he really needed me. I wasn't attracted to him physically. And I didn't really like him as a person, from what I knew of him, just seeing him around. But he kept following me around so much that I started going out with him. He told me about things that upset him, so I felt emotionally close to him, and I felt like he was mixed up and that he really needed me. That was attractive to me."

Lisa + Will

In exploring why she was attracted to her partner, she talks about her own craving to be needed:

> "I guess taking care of him gave me a sense of security in some way, because I was really insecure in myself. I never felt important in my family."

Another ACMI describes the conflicting emotions caused by being a caretaker:

> "Sometimes I feel that my wife is enjoying herself too much, being in touch with her childlike side. I'm jealous that I'm not. And I also resent the fact that this puts me in the parenting role, when her child cries out at me. It's like the double-edged sword: In a way I like giving comfort, and then I resent it, resent being there for her. Why can't *I* be like that? I don't allow myself to be in that position. If I am, I get too scared and say 'this isn't right.'"

Choosing Abusive Partners

Those of you who suffered physical and/or emotional abuse may find that you consistently pick an abusive partner. In such a relationship, you re-create your childhood experience. You live with the fear and with the blows to your self-esteem you grew up with.

As an ACMI, you may be prone to overlook how poorly you're being treated. You focus instead on your partner's pain. Furthermore, the abusive partner–like the alcoholic who sobers up from time to time–goes through periods of being loving and affectionate. If you lived with a parent who was prone to erratic behavior, you may have a tendency to put up with these swings in behavior. In your childhood, you may have been eternally hopeful that your disturbed parent would recover and become a consistently loving parent. In your adult relationships, you may hold false hope about your partner's ability to change. One ACMI who was involved in an abusive relationship says:

> "I guess I really thought he would change, but he didn't. He'd say he wanted to marry me, but he'd be going around sleeping with different people. I knew about this before we got married. He loved to come home and tell me about it. Then he'd be all sorry, and he'd cry, and he'd want me to forgive him. And of course I did, and always believed that he wouldn't do it again. But he *would* do it again, very soon after."

It frequently takes the ACMI a long time to decide that a partner is not going to change his or her abusive ways. One woman, whose partner was physically abusive, talks about ending the relationship after many years of abuse:

> "I just got to the point where I couldn't make myself believe he would change any more. It was a long process. At one point he hit me, and I got really upset. I told him that if he ever hit me again I would kill him, and I really made him believe it. And then I just decided I was leaving. I wasn't going to stick around and endure it any more."

Resisting Intimacy

Another typical choice for the ACMI is a partner who remains emotionally distant and unengaged. With such a person you can remain aloof and invulnerable yourself. This can be a place of safety for you, since you don't need to open up emotionally to your partner. One ACMI describes this type of relationship:

"I used to pick people who didn't seem to expect too much from me. They never got upset but they also didn't share much of what they thought and felt. After a while I'd start hammering at them to open up about their feelings. Of course, I didn't realize that I would have been scared to death if they had started to want more involvement with me."

There are a number of reasons why you, as an ACMI, would want to be in this type of relationship. You may fear that closeness will bring the same pain suffered in childhood. Or you may be afraid of losing your own boundaries. When asserting your needs and setting limits is difficult, you fear being engulfed by your partner's personality. A distant partner doesn't threaten your shaky boundaries.

Some ACMIs find themselves unable to form any sustained primary relationships. You might stay with a partner for a short period of time, but you remain unable to commit to a relationship of any duration. Here an ACMI talks about her tendency to run away from relationships:

"There have been times within this recent relationship that I've really gotten in touch with the fact that if I don't work on my stuff and try to deal with an intimate relationship, instead of running away from it when it gets hard, I probably will spend the rest of my life in and out of relationships. I'll never have the stability that I really would like."

Recognizing Your Patterns

Since these choices are often made unconsciously, you may find yourself very unhappy about being in such relationships. Consciously you seek a loving partner. You wish that you could be with someone who provides you with the intimacy you crave. However, on a less conscious level, you continue to accept what's familiar. Because of the negative conclusions you drew about yourself during your deprived childhood years, unconsciously you may feel you don't deserve a better relationship.

Lisa

Some of you, even after breaking off an unsatisfying relationship, continue the pattern. You find yourself caught up in yet another dysfunctional relationship. It's possible to repeat this pattern time and again, blinding yourself to the initial signs and subtle indications that this new person may be unable to form a close, healthy relationship.

For others, breaking out of an unfulfilling relationship marks the beginning of a profound realization that you *can* have and do deserve a more nurturing relationship. Such a shift usually comes after you start to understand how your family history made you vulnerable to this situation. With your eyes open to your patterns, you can start to change the nature of your relationships.

An ACMI talks about the turning point in her willingness to look at her past:

"I got involved, very briefly, with a woman who was emotionally abusive. Before I got involved with her I had no way of knowing that she would behave that way. And that really triggered a lot in me. I had known for years that I would have to do work around what had happened in my childhood, but I was afraid of touching it. I was so afraid of this 'thing,' this monster, that I didn't want to go near it."

The "Good Enough" Mate– Giving Up the Extremes

For some of you, even when you understand that you deserve and can have a healthy relationship, you're still bewildered by the question of what a "normal" relationship is. In your tendency to swing between extremes, you may find yourself thinking that if you're now saying "no" to abusive relationships, the only thing you can say "yes" to is an ideal and perfect relationship. As an ACMI, you may move back and forth in relationships between images of pain and deprivation and images of perfection. You may not be aware that you're thinking in extremes and thereby sabotaging your chance for a good relationship.

Like a Cinderella, as a child the ACMI often lives with images of the fairy godmother and the handsome prince. Some of you have reported that you frequently daydreamed that you were adopted and your real mother or father would some day come along and provide you with all the love and support that was lacking in your home environment. Or you may not have been as conscious of these types of dreams. You simply felt the pain of not having what you needed. Somewhere inside, you harbored hope of some day being given the love and attention that you so much needed.

The ACMI usually brings these childhood cravings into adult relationships. As you come to grips with your tendency to choose destructive or depriving relationships and begin to reach out for more nurturing partners, you often find yourself confused by the fact that what a partner can provide is finite and limited. Secretly your hope has been that once you got into a good relationship your mate could make up for all the deprivation you suffered as a child. You don't consciously and rationally say that this is what you want and expect, but at times you find yourself angry and disappointed with your partner when he or she doesn't meet all of your needs. You may find that your anger and disappointment are out of proportion.

When you encounter these feelings in your newer, healthier relationship, remember that your partner is as human and full of needs as you, and therefore cannot always come through for you. The child inside of you has some old longings that are quite understandable, but that can't always be fulfilled.

Self-Esteem and Self-Expression

Your family was probably unable to treat you in ways that would enhance your self-esteem. Most ACMIs come to adulthood with a deep sense of unworthiness. However, many of you aren't aware that it is this deeply rooted feeling that's at the core of your difficulty in finding and sustaining a satisfying relationship. Frequently you don't realize why you run away at the first mention of commitment. Or you don't understand why you pick one "loser" after another. Or you wonder why you tend to isolate yourself rather than reach out for the possibility of relationships.

How I used to be

As you begin the process of building your self-esteem, one of the most important elements is reclaiming your right to your emotions and needs. Being close to another human being requires an ability to express yourself fully with that other person. For a relationship to work, both people need to be in touch with, and communicate, their feelings and desires. In a lopsided relationship in which only one person communicates needs and the other responds, neither person is being fully themselves. But an equal give and take, a full expression of two human beings, is precisely what many of you are afraid of.

You learned early in life that your needs wouldn't be met. You found, in fact, that they would get you into trouble. And you learned that expressing sadness or fear or anger would simply bring you inappropriate and often painful responses from the adults in your life. Therefore you decided long ago not to share these intimate aspects of yourself with another person. Furthermore, most of you are so used to not sharing your feelings, and have cast yourself in a caretaker role for so long, that you may have trouble *knowing* what you actually feel. An ACMI describes her struggle to learn about her needs and to voice them:

> "My boyfriend let me know that he really wanted me to be more assertive. You know, that was the first time anybody ever told me that. It felt great. But even when I can get in touch with what I want, I still find myself holding back. I never got what I needed when I was a kid, so I just learned not even to bother to ask. I realize that's all part of having intimate relationships–letting the other person know what your needs are. That's been one of my main issues."

How can the ACMI change these ingrained patterns of behavior? The next section of the book will look at some practical ways to begin learning self-knowledge and self-expression, and to begin changing the nature of your relationships.

Part II

Turning the Past Around

"In the past I would try to fit other people's expectations of who they wanted me to be, try to be very agreeable and try not to have opinions that would be too different from other people's. And in love relationships, for a long time I would try to be who the other person wanted me to be. I was out of touch with what I wanted or what I needed. And I still find myself doing that. I still sometimes have a hard time deciding what I want to do for myself."

–An ACMI

5

Reclaiming Your Feelings

"A sense of identity–that's one thing I felt I had none of when I was growing up. I based everything I did in my life on what I thought I should do or what other people wanted me to do. I have an imagination that just amazes me about what I *think* I should do. I'm just now getting in touch with what I really want to do, and believing that it's okay, whatever it is. And it's still hard for me to feel good about that. I'm still looking over my shoulder to see what the reaction is going to be. Every time I make a decision, I have to think, 'What is this decision for? Is it for me? Is it something I really want to do? Or am I doing it for somebody else?'"

The first step in the journey toward recovering your "self" is to begin to look closely into yourself for all those missing needs and feelings. Fortunately, we're never able to fully suppress who we are. If you're determined to discover these disowned aspects of yourself, you'll find that you're able to do so. If you're someone who has tended to pay more attention to another person's needs than to your own, you may want to begin, in small and simple ways, to notice your own preferences, to tune in to your own rhythms and needs. It may be as simple as knowing which movie to see, or where to go for your vacation, or whether you feel more like going for a walk or lying down and taking a nap.

To allow yourself to notice these kinds of preferences marks the beginning of being able to acknowledge more important needs. If you are at this stage of learning, you will need to experiment with expressing these needs to people you're close to. This may sound very easy for those who are used to speaking up about what they want. But for someone who has built a life around putting others first, it can be a frightening thing to do.

Getting Started on Getting in Touch

When you're having a hard time getting in touch with your preferences, it's often useful to present yourself with a menu of choices. As you scan your menu of choices–for example, "what do I feel like doing today?" or "when my friend and I get together, what activity would I like to suggest?" it's useful to notice what inner responses you have to the items on your menu. For example, think about what subtle signals you experiencewhen you are looking at a restaurant menu, signals that tell you, "I would rather order this dish than that." Perhaps what happens when you hit upon the item that you want to order is a sudden feeling of excitement, or a sense of clarity–a coming into focus that suddenly says, "Yes, that's what I want!" You may be going down your list of choices with a generally uninterested feeling–"No, that's not it and that's not it." Then when something piques your interest, you sense a change inside of you, a little bit of aliveness that wasn't there before. By tuning in on your unique way of signaling "yes," you can learn to become more sensitive to your choices.

Another way of getting in touch with your preferences, particularly when you're trying to decide between two choices, is to use something arbitrary, like the flip of a coin. When you do the coin flip, saying "heads, I'll do this and tails I'll do that," and it comes up heads, notice your initial reaction. You may find that you feel a sense of pleasure or of disappointment at the outcome. You may realize that you actually had a preference you weren't in touch with. You may have been trying to make the decision on a strictly rational basis, weighing the pros and cons of each choice, but once you flipped the coin and the choice was supposedly made for you, then your emotional preference became apparent.

Another game is to imagine a perfect universe in which you may have anything and everything you want. By noticing where this fantasy takes you, you can look closely at your choices. You may be able to sense the nature and direction of your needs and translate these needs into a form where they can be met in reality.

For example, when you look at the fantasy you've formed, you may notice that it contains a lot more contact with people than you have now. Or your fantasy may involve more light-hearted activities; you may discover that you're wishing you had more room in your life to play. Or maybe your fantasy seems to contain a wide variety of interesting activities. You may realize that you've been keeping yourself understimulated, not pursuing those activities you'd like to get involved in. While your fantasy of a perfect universe in which you have total control over everything that you want is not likely to materialize, you can use your fantasies as a way of getting in touch with longings you might be able to fulfill.

Feelings and the Body

Experience begins in our bodies. Many people find this a surprising thought, but a feeling is a physical event. Just as you feel physical pain when you put your hand on a hot stove, emotions, too, are physiological events. For example, we know that crying involves tears and sounds and changes in breathing patterns. Also, when someone is suppressing a strong feeling, like the need to cry, it takes a physical effort to stifle that feeling. If you try very hard not to cry, you may tighten a lot of muscles in your face and throat and restrict your breathing to hold back the tears. Or think about how your heart may have been pounding with fear when you stood up to give a speech, or perhaps your mouth suddenly got very dry.

In becoming sophisticated in noticing your feelings, a good first step is to begin to tune in to what's going on in your body. When you ask yourself, "What am I feeling?" and you don't get a clear answer to that question, ask yourself, "What's going on inside my body?" Take an inventory. Notice what's going on with your breathing–is it shallow or deep, is it rapid or slow? Are you aware of your heart? Is it beating slowly or fast? What is your temperature like? Are you sweating? Are you cold and clammy? Are you trembling? Is any part of your body clenched or stiff?

Some of your signals may be subtle. You might not find your heart racing furiously or your fists clenched.

Instead you may notice a little bit of tightness in your throat, or you hands turning cold.

Over time, you'll learn to connect these sensations with feelings. For example, you may discover that you tighten up the muscles in your neck and shoulders whenever you're holding back a particular feeling. Or perhaps your stomach knots up. As you begin to understand the vocabulary of your own body, you'll be able to move faster from the question, "What am I feeling?" to the answer, "I'm feeling angry" (or sad, or excited, or fearful).

Feeling and Not Feeling

As you learn to connect feelings with physical sensations, you'll get better at noticing the ways in which you suppress your feelings. For example, a friend of yours asks to borrow your car. You agree that she can use it as long as she puts in some gas before returning it. Later that day, after she's returned the car, you find that the gas tank reads empty. A few minutes later, as you're driving around looking for an open gas station, you notice that your jaw is clenched and your shoulders are very tight. You know that you have a great deal of trouble allowing yourself to be angry. You realize that your body is sending a signal to you that's characteristic of how you feel when you're angry. You then remember that you had a very brief flash of anger when you saw the empty gas gauge. You had immediately tried to talk yourself out of your anger by telling yourself that it really wasn't important. You now realize that your body is telling you that you're quite irritated with your friend. As you allow yourself to experience some of this anger, you may find that your clenched jaw and tight shoulders let go a little bit. When you remind yourself that you'll be seeing your friend tomorrow and can talk to her about it then, the tension in your body lets go even a little more. It's a relief to acknowledge to yourself what you feel and to know you'll be able to talk about it.

Fear of Feelings

Some of you may find that simply attempting to tune in to your feelings and needs doesn't seem to elicit them. You may find, after trying hard to listen to yourself, that nobody seems to be speaking up. When this is the case, you're probably dealing with a great deal of fear. You've protected yourself for so long by denying your feelings that now it's difficult for you to gain access to them. If this is true, the emotion of fear is the place to start.

It may be helpful to *assume* that you're frightened about reclaiming your feelings. You can then test this assumption by looking for signs that you're afraid. For example, in any situation that might call for you to express yourself–stating a preference about activities or speaking up about a feeling–you find yourself blank. If you tune more closely into that blankness, you may find that what you are really saying is: "This is too scary. I'm scared to know what I want. I'm scared to know what I'm feeling."

Given your difficult background, this is a perfectly understandable response to your first attempts to counteract your old programming. If you can simply feel your fear, you're taking an important first step. Since so many of you grew up with a great deal of fear, you had to find ways of tuning out that fear in order to function adequately. If you can begin to acknowledge the fear you carry within you, this is a major step toward reaching past it to the rest of your feelings.

Feelings and Moods

Sometimes you may find it difficult to be in touch with a specific feeling. However, you might be aware of being in a certain mood on a given day. For example, you may be feeling depressed, restless, irritable, anxious, or bored. Moods like these are often a coverup for specific feelings lying underneath–for example, depression can cover up anger. A mood can tip you off about what you're feeling. Sometimes it's enough to ask yourself, "What am I feeling underneath this mood?" At other times it can be useful to ask yourself questions such as: "When did the mood begin? What recent interactions may have set it off? What thoughts was I thinking earlier, when the mood began? When in the past have I felt this sort of mood and what kinds of situations caused it?"

Over time, you may learn that you use certain moods to cover up certain feelings. For example, you may frequently have a hard time allowing yourself to feel angry. Instead you may lapse into depression. If you know what sort of feelings you typically cover up with a certain mood, this will help you get in touch with the underlying feelings.

One way you can discover the feeling underneath one of these moods is to exaggerate the mood. For example, if you're feeling restless and you wonder what's underneath that feeling, it may help to pace about your room and notice what comes to the surface when you let yourself express the restlessness. You may find other feelings beginning to emerge. For example, the restless feeling might begin to turn into anger. As you continue pacing, ask yourself about the source of your anger. Images or thoughts may filter in: the mechanic who's holding your car hostage this weekend, a friend who's recently stepped on your toes, frustration with your job, or dissatisfaction with your relationships.

Another example is when you're feeling blue. You could curl up in a chair, hugging yourself, letting go into the mood. By staying with this for a while, you may begin to feel more sad, perhaps even tearful. When you ask yourself about the sadness, images of happy couples may point to loneliness. Or perhaps a friend's face will come into your mind and you'll realize you're feeling pushed away by something she recently said. Or perhaps you'll think of your work and find you're disappointed about not getting an interesting assignment you'd been hoping for. This process of allowing feelings to intensify can help to make the nature of them clearer.

Feelings and Boundaries

 "I was totally tuned in to her. I mean, I knew her mood from the other room. I needed to for my survival."

Many of the ACMI's problems in contacting feelings stem from a childhood failure to complete the process of developing a personal identity. You may have trouble recognizing where your feelings stop and the other person's begin. Your sense of identity hinges on your ability to recognize who you are, separate and distinct from other people.

You may have grown up with a parent who was unable to clearly distinguish the boundary between what was inside of him or her and what was occurring outside. A hallucination is an extreme example of such a boundary confusion. A more common example of this might be your parent accusing you of being angry when, in fact, he or she is the one who's angry. *Mom did this a lot—still does*

Those ACMIs who take on caretaker roles have great difficulty stepping back from such an experience and retaining a sense of their own emotional state. If you have difficulties in this area, you may find that you feel depressed when you're with someone who's depressed, and you feel anxious when you're around somebody who's anxious. A complaint that you commonly voice is "I always lose myself when I'm around other people. It's hard for me to feel my *own* emotions and needs. I'm just too sensitive." As an ACMI, you probably *are* quite sensitive. This sensitivity, while it can involve a certain kind of fragility, can also become one of your greatest assets–if you learn how to use it correctly. Your attunement to other people's feelings and needs can either be used as a vehicle for avoiding contact with yourself or as a valuable gift that can lead you back home to your self. By learning to listen as carefully to your own signals as you do to others', you can hone your own sensitivity as a tool for tuning into yourself. And once you're aware of your own feelings and needs, you'll be more able to form close bonds with others without having your identity merge with theirs.

As an example of how this process can work *for* you, consider how you read the subtle physical cues another person offers. Often without realizing it, you are picking up almost subliminal messages–such as a slight change in tone of voice, an almost unnoticeable movement, a glance, a pause. Your survival once depended on this kind of early warning system:

"I would often just be silent, waiting for a clue to her mood to find out how to feed her. I was like a straight man in a comedy act. And I always knew what my lines were. I knew just what to do."

You may have learned to pick up and respond to these subtle signals more rapidly than a person who grew up in a safer environment. If you can shift your focus onto your *own* signals, you may be able to get to your emotions by picking up your own physical cues.

There are other ways to help yourself, too. If you have friends who are close enough to provide feedback, ask them to point out when you're overlooking your needs, or when they see in your face a bit of feeling that you seem to be out of touch with. For example, a friend might let you know that you have a sad expression on your face right now. This may enable you to tune in to that feeling.

If you don't have access through friendships to this kind of feedback, individual or group therapy may be of help here, too. Therapy can provide you with a setting to receive feedback about feelings which are visible to others, but which you may be out of touch with.

Different methods work for each of you at this point. For some of you, feelings may be more available when you're alone or watching a movie or listening to music. For others, throwing yourself into contact with people and seeing what's evoked in you is more effective in bringing your feelings to the surface.

Learning to be in touch with your feelings is an important first step toward communicating with other people. Knowing what's going on inside of you–being able to communicate with *yourself* about your internal world–is a necessary prerequisite for communicating with others about your feelings and needs. Using some of the techniques I've suggested, you can make getting in touch with yourself a less mysterious process. Once you've learned some of the skills involved, it will grow easier to know what you are feeling in any situation. This in turn will put you more in touch with your needs.

Getting Comfortable With Your Feelings

At this point you may also notice some changes that make you uncomfortable. Perhaps you'll be more easily angered than you had previously been. Maybe you'll find yourself feeling like crying far more frequently. Or maybe you'll be in touch with how scary many of your contacts with other people are, where before you may have just braved it out by being stoic. This is because you're signaling your dormant feelings, telling them that there's now room for them to exist.

As you begin to come more alive, as you start to declare yourself a person apart from other people's needs, it is inevitable that this major shift will leave you feeling fairly stirred up. You've had little experience in dealing with these kinds of emotions. Before, you just suppressed them. The growing-up years and the years of early adulthood are normally a time to develop your interactive skills. But you stayed away from this kind of give-and-take. While many of your peers were probably learning to express their needs more surely and accurately, you were spending your energy trying to sidestep your own needs. What you're discovering now is that you have some catching up to do. This can be a hard phase for you. As a beginner, you're awkward and uncomfortable with your unfamiliar feelings. You're also not used to expressing them to other people. As a result, you may find that you don't always express yourself in ways that are easy for others to understand.

Some of you have talked about your fear that expressing what you want would only lead to a conflict with the other person, ending up in a stormy and hostile scene. This is the ghost of your past telling you that if you express yourself, things will end up in chaos. In your past you had no model for constructive conflict.

Even if you and a friend differ on what you want and each of you feels strongly about it, there can be positive negotiating about how to solve the dilemma. Taking it a step further, even if the discussion becomes heated, you can, over time, learn to deal with anger—your own and others'—without being frightened that it might escalate into an abusive situation. Viewing a situation in extremes (if I say one little thing, it will lead to this huge scene) is part of the all-or-nothing, black-and-white thinking that a person develops growing up in a family where unpredictable and frightening behavior was the norm.

> "I've gotten better about it, but for a while, my anger was really scary to me because anger meant you destroyed things. It's taken me years to learn differently."
>
> *
>
> "I believe I grew up in a war zone. You know, it was on a daily basis that these things happened. There was a lot of violence."

The dysfunctional attitudes you carry will probably show up in one of two opposing way. You might be timid and self-effacing in your approach to other people, minimizing your needs and apologizing for bringing them up. Or, in contrast, you may use far more force than the situation warrants.

There are a number of ways to provide yourself the room you need to fumble about with these new feelings and behaviors. One thing that has helped many ACMIs is sitting down from time to time with their mate or close friends to talk about what they're going through. If the people close to you understand that you're attempting to retrieve parts of yourself that haven't seen the light of day since childhood, they will be more understanding if your first attempts to express yourself are a little awkward.

At this stage, a therapeutic setting can also be useful. It can allow you to experiment, with the help of a skilled therapist, in a context where people come specifically to deal with such issues. Many of you report that both the one-to-one attention of individual therapy and the support of a group struggling with similar issues eases the turmoil of this particular phase of recovery.

Ultimately, as you struggle through changing these lifelong patterns, you may have to accept that some friends might not stick by you. Frequently those who don't remain your friends are those who themselves lack the internal flexibility to shift the roles the two of you are used to, and to allow you room to explore new ones. Most of you will find that there *are* some good friends who care enough to go through a bit of turmoil with you. And often those relationships will become deeper and richer than before.

6

If You're Mad,
I Must Be Bad–
Building Self-Esteem

"It's hard for me to really believe in myself. There's some part of me that just doesn't believe I'm love-able. I know I am, but I guess no matter how much I know it, there's still some part of me that doesn't believe it. And it affects me in almost every way."

Chapters 1 and 4 discussed the serious difficulties the ACMI has in achieving and maintaining a sense of self-worth. While growing up with a great deal of deprivation and abuse, you may have harbored a childlike belief that you deserved the poor treatment you were getting. It's common for children who are receiving inadequate parenting to blame themselves. They assume that their large and powerful parents are in control of what they're doing, and if love isn't given, it must not be deserved.

As you grow older and see your parents a little more clearly, your maturing mind begins to recognize their difficulties and limitations. By the time you're an adult, you're able to say to yourself that mom or dad was emotionally disturbed and therefore unable to provide the loving parenting you needed. This knowledge, however, doesn't always filter down to influence the little child who still lives inside you. It's necessary to talk to that hidden child and to recognize how much that child's feelings color your view of yourself and the world around you.

Most of you who struggle with issues of low self-esteem would say that of course you are as worthy as the next person and certainly don't deserve to suffer. You can probably name some of your strengths, as well as weaknesses, and acknowledge that *everyone* has strengths and weaknesses. However, on an emotional level, you may not believe this. Your behavior in the world will show that you don't have faith in yourself. You may find yourself, for instance, placing yourself in a one-down and fearful position in social situations. You may limit yourself because of your fears of other people's judgments and rejections. You may set your sights quite low in your career in spite of being intelligent and industrious. You may find yourself suffering from bouts of depression. You may sabotage love relationships or job opportunities. There are many symptoms of low self-esteem. You may want to consider for a moment some of the forms in which your sense of inadequacy shows up in your life.

Your Insecure Inner Child

How can you begin to spot the insecure child within you? Perhaps you tend to be insecure in certain social situations. For example, you may be nervous about an upcoming event in which you're going to meet new people. If you listen carefully to that nervousness, you'll be able to hear the words that accompany the fear. Perhaps you're saying to yourself: "I'm not going to have anything to say. I'm going to be awkward and uninteresting. These people are going to think I'm a real klutz." If you listen further to what you're saying, you may even find that you're supporting this prediction with evidence from past experiences. You may have some memories of feeling nervous and awkward in previous social encounters. Now you're saying to yourself, "Since I couldn't think of anything to say that other time, I won't be able to carry on a conversation this time." So you're predicting how you'll behave in the future based on your past performance. You're also guessing what the opinion of others will be about how you conduct yourself. If you don't actively intervene in this pattern, it will gain its own momentum and become a self-fulfilling prophecy: because you're telling yourself you'll be awkward, you will approach the situation with a great deal of fear and insecurity. This fear may very well *cause* you to be tongue-tied and tense.

The child in you who's running the show believes that the lack of love in your past proves that you're unloveable. If that's the truth, then of course these new people you're about to meet won't find you loveable.

The adult in you senses the anxiety of that inner child and translates that fear into terms that are a little more rational for you as an adult. For example, since you don't assume—or even necessarily seek—a deep, loving relationship with each person you meet, the adult in you doesn't say, "Oh dear, these new people aren't going to love me." Instead, you translate your concern into the idea that in some way you're going to fail to make a comfortable introductory contact with these people. So you've translated "I'm not loveable" into "I'm socially awkward." Instead of telling yourself, "I'll be rejected because I am totally worthless," you tell yourself, "They won't want to get together with me again because I didn't have anything interesting to say."

In order to break through this vicious cycle of anxiety and inhibition, you need to see through your adult ways of cloaking your insecurity and look into the mind and feelings of that child within you. If you can begin to do this, you'll be able to soothe yourself by seeing that there isn't nearly as much at stake in this situation as that child believes. That hungry, unloved child in you is seeking all the care you never got—and expecting all the rejection and abuse you did receive. Approaching any new, unknown person in your world revives that craving and that specter once again.

If you can acknowledge that your rejected, hungry child is really the source of your anxiety, you may be able to stop worrying about adult matters, such as carrying on a conversation, and turn your attention to comforting that child. You'll need to give some thought to what kind of comfort your inner child would respond to. Perhaps it's a reassurance that you are loveable; perhaps it's a reminder that you're safe now, that you won't allow the severe rejection of the past to be repeated. You may then find that you can approach social situations with less anxiety.

Self-Talk

There's another way to help yourself reduce this kind of social anxiety. You can change the way you talk to yourself about an upcoming event. The more often you say to yourself, "I'm going to be awkward and tongue-tied," the more anxious you will become. All of us create feelings in ourselves by the words that we say to ourselves. A simple example of this would be saying to yourself, "Oh my God, I'm going to be late for work!" and suddenly feeling quite anxious. If you say to yourself, "I need to hurry a bit to get to work," you will probably feel a little less anxious than you would with the first statement. If you want to make yourself feel *really* bad, say to yourself, "Oh my God, I'm going to be late for work and if I don't make it, it's going to be really horrible–I'm such an idiot for having gotten such a late start." In response, you'll probably have a mixture of feelings: anxiety, perhaps some depression, feeling weighed down by the judgments against yourself, maybe even feeling close to tears.

In the same way, when you approach a social situation you can say things to yourself that will make you either more or less anxious. Instead of making drastic predictions about how poorly the event is going to go, you can anticipate positive outcomes. In addition, you can remind yourself how much your inner child tends to blow things out of proportion. For example, you may say to yourself: "It'll be fun to meet some new people. I imagine that I'll find them interesting and have lots to say to them. If, however, it turns out that we don't have enough in common, it's just one social situation among hundreds of meetings with people that I'll have over a lifetime, and therefore the outcome of this particular one isn't that important." In this way, you put the adult within you in charge of the upcoming event: you take an optimistic stance about the possibility of enjoying the meeting. You also remind the child within you that no matter how it goes this is a rather minor event and not a replay of growing up with a disturbed parent.

In this fashion, you give yourself the opportunity to approach these situations with less anxiety, and therefore increase your chances of having a successful encounter. If you're then able to enjoy the meeting, you'll be less fearful the next time such an occasion arises. Instead of perpetuating a negative cycle, you can begin a cycle of positive prediction and positive outcome.

If You're Holding on to Low Self-Esteem

As you consider challenging some of these patterns of low self-esteem, you may find yourself feeling reluctant to tackle these issues. This may be a signal that you have an investment in maintaining some negative beliefs about yourself. It's important not to interpret this resistance as an indication that these methods can't work for you, or take it as another reason to feel badly about yourself. There are good reasons for you to be attached to the negative beliefs about yourself. In the past, these beliefs operated to protect you in important ways. Most people find that they don't give up their negative self-image very readily. If it were easy to do, you would already have done so. It may help to look at how your negative self-image has been your friend.

Your negative thoughts about yourself probably functioned as protection from the childhood pain of parental rejection. Most children have difficulty facing the stark reality of being unloved. Children often blame themselves for this lack of love. As painful as this self-blame is, it can be a way of gleaning a small amount of hope and control in the situation. The reasoning goes: "If I'm to blame for the lack of love and attention, then perhaps there's something I can *do* to win it. Therefore, the situation isn't entirely hopeless. If I'm just good enough, if I can just figure out what they want from me, if I just try hard enough, then perhaps I can win their approval." In this way, hanging on to a shred of hope, the unloved child can continue to believe that the parent who is failing him or her is actually *capable* of giving the nurturing that's so desperately needed. To give up this self-blame, therefore, is tantamount to giving up all hope of ever having what you need. It means accepting that you aren't causing the situation and there's nothing you can do to change it. (Chapter 2 described the "fix-it" compulsion many ACMIs feel when faced with a friend's problem.)

As a child, this helplessness was too painful to face. You may have protected yourself by taking the blame. As an adult, when you begin to uncover this protective maneuver, you may find that you have to face the deep pain of never having gotten the kind of care that you needed. Facing this pain and recovering from it can ultimately lead you toward a greater capacity for close relationships. However, you may find yourself reluctant to experience the sadness that comes with recognizing that the child in you will never have parents who provide adequate love and nurturing. You may find yourself tempted to continue to see yourself as inadequate rather than face the fact that your childhood is over.

Another function of holding on to low self-esteem involves protection against taking healthy risks in current relationships. It serves as a reason to avoid taking these risks. If you begin to feel more confident about yourself, you'll reach out in ways that you previously haven't. You'll set goals for yourself that you haven't dared entertain before. Moving on to new territory of any sort always involves a danger: while you may sometimes get what you want, you may also have to handle disappointment. It feels safer to not make the attempt. Furthermore, each time you challenge that negative self-image and take a risk that doesn't work out, you'll probably have a tendency to blame yourself again. So, if you don't risk anything, you can't "fail."

After recognizing your motivations for holding on to your old self-image, you may find yourself more willing to change. Since many of you have grown up feeling that you had little choice about how you felt about yourself, it can be an exciting prospect to realize that you can learn to build your self-esteem. You can start the process by listening to your inner child and by learning to talk to yourself in positive ways. While learning how to feel better about yourself does take consistent and dedicated work, it can be quite a relief to realize that it can be done.

Moving From Guilt to Compassion

Many ACMIs have a hard time understanding the difference between guilt and compassion. Guilt is the feeling that because the other person is in pain, you are doing something wrong. Compassion is the ability to feel for the other person, to care about the fact that he is in pain, without assuming that you are the cause of the pain or have the responsibility for getting rid of it. In order to develop the ability to be compassionate, you must be willing to accept the limits of what you can or can't do for another person. As ACMIs, many of you grew up wishing you could solve an insoluble problem. You felt inadequate because you couldn't heal a wounded parent. It became difficult for you to witness another person's discomfort without feeling inadequate.

The key to accepting the limits of what you can do for another person lies in developing a tolerance to certain uncomfortable feelings such as helplessness and sadness. Most ACMIs find that they want to feel in control in most situations. It takes practice to learn to tolerate a feeling of helplessness. You may feel helpless sitting with a friend who is in pain, knowing that while you can comfort her, you can't take away her pain or solve her problems. Often sadness accompanies the feeling of helplessness. You feel sorry that you can't fix the problem, can't take away your friend's discomfort. As you develop an ability to feel compassion rather than guilt, you'll find that you are more and more comfortable accepting the limits of what you can offer. You'll recognize that the empathy you do offer is quite a gift in itself.

There are some specific steps you can take to develop your ability to respond with empathy rather than with a "fix-it" attitude. You'll first need to envision some typical situations in which you're called upon for support. Then jot down a fix-it and empathic response to each situation. For example:

Fix-it response	**Empathic response**

Betty's unhappiness about her job:

"Why don't you quit your job and look for a better one?"	"Boy, it sure sounds like it's rough for you at work these days."

John's sadness about his marriage breakup:

"Well it's probably for the best, since you weren't happy with the relationship. Don't feel so hopeless. As soon as you're feeling up to it, I can fix you up with my friend Martha."	"Gee, it must be really painful being alone after all these years. I'm sorry you're going through such a hard time."

Jane's fear about upcoming surgery:

"There's really nothing to be scared of; they say it's a pretty safe procedure. I saw an article about it that I could bring you."	"I can see how scared you're feeling. I guess that any surgery, no matter how "routine" the doctors say it is, is a little frightening for the patient. Can you tell me exactly what it is that's making you the most apprehensive about it?"

Once you have your list, think about what statements you need to make to yourself to counteract your usual tendency to avoid the helplessness and sadness of others' pain. Your list might include such statements as:

- "The best help I can give is just to be there for him/her."
- "I can be of help, but I can't solve his/her problem."
- "Emotional understanding is the biggest gift I can give."
- "Some of the sadness and helplessness I'm feeling is my old (family) pain."

As you come to accept what you can and can't give, you'll find an increase in your self acceptance and self-love. As this occurs, you'll begin to feel more deserving of a satisfying life.

7

Overcoming Blocks to Risk-Taking

Chapter 4 discussed some of the dilemmas you'll encounter when you start to express yourself after years
of inexperience. To begin with, most of you are trying
to break certain old equations. At the same time, you're
proceeding mostly on faith. You have decided to experiment with the notion that not everybody will reject your
needs or retaliate if you express some anger. However,
since you're conditioned to expect negative responses,
you'll approach these situations with a lot of fear. You
may therefore bring upon yourself the negative outcome you expect.

If you do engage in this "self-fulfilling prophecy"
behavior, you may end up retreating once again to the
old belief that it's no use trying to express yourself.
Therefore, you must add to the new equation that
sometimes people won't be receptive to your expressing yourself. This lack of receptivity may simply have to
do with their own issues or it may have something to do
with *how* you approach people rather than the fact that
you *did* approach them.

How Negative Assumptions Block Risk-Taking

The risk of expressing your needs and feelings seems immeasurably greater when you bring negative assumptions to the interaction. For example, if you assume that the other person is hostile or at best uninterested, you're not going to risk much. If you assume that he or she is selfish or insensitive, that too will tend to discourage direct communication. While these assumptions served to protect you as a child, they are now in the way of expressing the real you.

It's time now to examine the basic kinds of negative assumptions that may keep you from risk-taking.

Personalizing

One error that people frequently make when communicating needs and feelings has to do with personalizing the problem. Personalizing means assuming that other people's behavior is always determined by their feelings toward you. For example, you may assume they act the way they do because they don't care about you or they dislike you.

As an ACMI, you felt responsible for everything that went right or wrong at home. The mood swings of an unstable parent always seemed related to something you did or failed to do. Little wonder that, as an adult, you assume that the feelings and reactions of others all have to do with you.

As a child, experiencing yourself as the center of your universe, it may have been difficult for you to understand that the inadequate parenting you received was not aimed at you, and was not an attempt to hurt or punish you. Only when you got somewhat older could you see that your disturbed parent's behavior had little to do with you or what you deserved.

The antidote to personalizing is to take a step back and consider the possibility that the other person's behavior may have little or nothing to do with his or her feelings toward you. It may well be an expression of feelings, needs, pain, conditioning, and history that is completely unrelated to you. You're probably not being singled out. Consider the case of the friend who keeps you waiting each time you get together. There's an excellent chance that he or she is chronically late for every engagement. People have enduring habits that have nothing to do with you. People have hurts, priorities, yearnings, and losses that you certainly have not caused. You are not the center of *their* universe, only your own.

When you're feeling responsible for or hurt by someone's behavior, you can do two things:

1. Assume that you are probably personalizing.
2. Make a list of at least five explanations for their behavior that *have nothing to do with you.*

Global Labelling

Another assumption that you might make about others involves blanket condemnation. You protect yourself from hurt and rejection by rejecting others first. Global labels make other people "bad" so you can feel less vulnerable to their reactions. Bad, in this instance, is often expressed in a more sophisticated manner, such as inconsiderate, selfish, thoughtless, lazy, boorish, insensitive...the list is endless.

In taking this stance, you have moved away from focusing on a specific behavior that intrudes on you or that doesn't give you what you need. Instead, you are making assumptions about the other person's character. Global labels close the door on any curiosity you might have about the other person's behavior and on any real mutual attempt at problem solving. Basically you're saying, "They're bad, to hell with them."

ACMIs who have been verbally abused and criticized have a tendency themselves to put negative labels on others. It's difficult to refrain from doing unto others what was done unto you. The antidote to global labelling is empathy. As an ACMI, a strength (and liability) is your ability to identify with the other person's feelings. This empathy will help you imagine how difficult it would be to hear blanket judgments, and to learn not to fall back on them.

Self-Fulfilling Prophecy

The negative assumptions you make when approaching the other person are essentially ways of attempting to protect yourself. One danger of these negative assumptions is that you'll create a self-fulfilling prophecy: you'll generate the very negativity that you suspect lies within the other person. In other words, if you approach the other person in a manner that imples that he or she will deliberately hurt you, you're likely to elicit a defensive response. You may read the lack of receptivity as proof that your assumption was correct.

Healthy assertiveness involves maintaining a basically positive stance about both your own and the other person's loveability. As soon as you recognize the tendency toward negative assumptions in an encounter, step back. If you were about to excuse yourself and say something in a timid voice, tell yourself to speak up. No apology is needed if the problem you are addressing is a real one to you. Your needs are just as important as those of the person you're approaching. On the other hand, if you were about to charge angrily into a conversation, remember that the other person may react politely and helpfully if you present your problem as a shared one. It is often not easy to maintain a positive approach when you didn't grow up in a family where people treated each other with continued care and respect. It will probably take some effort to challenge the automatic assumptions about yourself and other people which you fall into. But if you can recognize your assumptions, you have taken the first step toward reassessing and changing them.

Trying Out New Behavior

In those instances when there's time to think about an exchange with another person before it actually happens, you may want to listen to yourself to see how the *old* pattern would be applied. For example, perhaps you have a roommate you're very fond of. She has a close friend who comes over frequently to visit. Very often when you arrive home you find your roommate—call her Bonnie—and her friend—call her Judy—sitting at the kitchen table engaged in a quiet, intimate conversation. They seem quite engrossed in what they're talking about and hardly notice your presence. As this frequently happens when Judy visits, you've begun to feel awkward and left out. Not only would you like to join in and get to know Judy better, but at times you need to be in the kitchen and you feel like you're intruding. You wish they would reach out to you in some way, inviting you to participate in the conversation.

At this point, your old behavior would be to say to yourself, "Well, Judy isn't really *my* friend, she's *Bonnie's* friend, and the two of them seem to be enjoying their conversation very much. I wouldn't want to do anything to disrupt their dialogue. It's a really nice thing for Bonnie that she has this close friend, and I certainly want her to feel comfortable about hanging out in the kitchen talking to her."

This is an example of how attuned you are to others' real or imagined needs. You figure that they're doing exactly what they want to be doing and that for you to introduce yourself into the picture would cause them some discomfort. In fact, what you are doing is pushing away your desire for contact, your wish to be included, and depriving yourself of what could potentially become a nice threesome. If you look underneath the denial of your needs, you may find a part of you that is suggesting you're somehow not desirable. You may be assuming that because they're enjoying each other they have no need for you.

To the degree that you aren't in touch with your own worth, it's difficult to believe that other people see you as a worthwhile human being. Standing in the kitchen listening to Bonnie and Judy, you have an opportunity to challenge those beliefs. It may be frightening, but you can make yourself a cup of tea and join them at the kitchen table with a simple, "Mind if I join you?" And then see what happens. This is a scary moment because your past says, "My wish to make contact may very well be rejected."

This moment of dealing with the unknown is hard for you to tolerate. You fill the void with the ghosts of your past and you expect to get hurt. With your antennae out to pick up any signals of possible rejection, you may read any momentary awkwardness on their part as a sign that they don't want to talk with you. You may find it difficult to give them, and yourself, time to shift gears and find a common ground.

For a while, conversation may flow less smoothly than it did when the two of them were talking. You may personalize this, assuming it means that they don't want to be with you. Or you may falsely label Bonnie and Judy as being rude people, who aren't trying to make you feel comfortable with them. Thus, your fear may lead you to behave in such a way that it's difficult to make contact with you. The conversation may remain awkward because you're having diffuculty letting it develop.

In such an instance you may silently declare the experiment a disaster and leave the kitchen rather hurriedly, vowing never again to "butt in." But the truth is, you created the very experience you expected. You ran away before the new threesome even had a chance.

Another option would be to tell Bonnie about your feelings after Judy leaves. You would tell her that sometimes when she and Judy are talking in such an involved and animated way in the kitchen you'd like to join them, but you're afraid of disrupting their conversation. Bonnie seems quite surprised and reassures you wholeheartedly that she and Judy would love to have you join them. She adds that, in fact, earlier that evening Judy had asked her how the two of you were getting along, and Bonnie told her how much she was enjoying rooming with you.

There are two points at which this exchange may be very hard for you. First, you might be afraid to approach Bonnie about the subject. Because of your fear, you might present your concern in a manner that is difficult to hear. You might, for instance, cover up your fear with belligerence, perhaps blaming Bonnie for the problem. You'd say to her, "Hey, you know, when you and Judy sit in the kitchen talking like that, you make me feel like a stranger in my own house. Why don't you ever include me?" If you approach Bonnie with this sort of an accusation, chances are you'll get back a defensive response.

Secondly, if you're able to deliver the initial question in a more gentle fashion and Bonnie has a chance to respond warmly to your concern, you may decide not to believe her reassurance. You'd say to yourself, "Well what else could she have said when I asked a question like that!" and dismiss what may be an authentic invitation. So remind yourself before approaching Bonnie that the exchange will go better if you assume she'll be receptive to you.

This example illustrates just one of the many types of day-to-day exchanges in which old fears and assumptions can block your desire for contact and intimacy. These patterns show up in your choice of mates and friends, and in how you view your needs and rights within your relationships. By observing how you interact with the people in your life, the fallout from your past can become more clear to you. This will give you an opportunity to try out new, more self-affirming approaches to relationships.

8

A Program of Graduated Risk-Taking

The previous four chapters have talked about the difficulty most ACMIs have in knowing what they're feeling, in expressing needs, and in setting limits with others. They offered some suggestions on how to get in touch with your feelings, and showed how you can shape your interactions through your ability or inability to assert yourself. Becoming skillfull in these areas is a little bit like an athlete developing his or her ability in a particular sport. It takes disciplined and methodical training, constantly building upon what one has previously learned. And just as the athlete must build up his strength slowly in order to avoid injury, a key to improving your relationships with other people is to make the necessary changes gradually.

This may seem frustrating at first. As you begin to understand some of your dysfunctional patterns, you'll probably want to change the ways you interact with others. You need to keep in mind that while you may understand *how* your relationships need to be improved, you probably lack some of the necessary skills to make these changes. So just as the novice skier would be foolhardy to start on an advanced slope, you must give yourself time to practice the basics. If you rush this process, you are likely, like the skier, to fall down so often that you'll feel like giving up the endeavor altogether.

The key to acquiring the skills that childhood didn't provide lies in carefully choosing the level of risk you're prepared to take. Like the skier who accepts the fact that some falling is inevitable and who is taught the safest ways to fall, it's important for you to learn how to minimize your chances of getting hurt. One important way of protecting yourself is to learn the art of creating a fallback position.

Preparing a Fallback Position

A fallback position is an internal safe place to return to if you're upset with the outcome of your experiment. Think of yourself as that beginning skier who has spent the morning out on the slopes and now needs a warm cabin, a hot lunch, and a change of clothes. The fallback position is a positive and supportive perspective that you create in advance. It's a message from the sturdiest and healthiest part of yourself to the scared child within you who needs comfort when an experiment proves stressful.

The fallback position contains your knowledge of what you set out to do and why it was positive for you to do it. It defines your experiment as a success no matter what the particular outcome. For example, if it's difficult for you to tell a friend that you're feeling hurt, simply telling your friend how you feel is already a triumph for you regardless of how she responds. If it's difficult for you to say no to a friend who keeps asking you to baby-sit, then setting that limit with her is great progress no matter how she responds to it. However, when you take that risk, if the other person responds defensively or with a display of emotion that's difficult for you to manage, you may define the risk as a failure. In truth, your discomfort with the reaction that you've gotten doesn't mean you've failed. So your fallback position should contain a statement like: "It's great that you took that risk regardless of how Mary responded to what you had to say. You're being very gutsy to experiment with new ways of interacting. Your willingness to take this risk will make your relationships better." It's important to have this fallback position very clear in your mind. It may help to write it down so that you can remind yourself periodically of the positive nature of your efforts.

Picking the Appropriate
Level of Risk

Aside from preparing a safety net to fall into should the interaction becomes stressful, there are four other ways you can regulate the amount of risk in any given inter-action:

1. deciding who to speak up with;
2. what content to address;
3. how often to speak up; and
4. how intimately to speak.

1. Who Should You Speak Up With?

If you think about it, you'll realize that you find certain people more frightening than others. For some of you, it's easier to express your feelings and needs to people you hardly know. For others, it's easier to express yourself to intimate friends. Some people find it easier to be forthcoming with men, and others with women. In some cases, the ease of contact has to do with certain characteristics of the other person. Maybe a gentle person seems safer to you, or a person who is assertive and strong. If you can begin to sort out who you feel more comfortable with, you can gather a great deal of information which you'll find useful when structuring levels of risk.

2. How Risky Is the Topic?

Another factor to consider in taking risks is an assessment of how likely you are to create conflict. You might feel pretty comfortable expressing yourself to a particular person. But even if you consider that person low-risk, you may also be aware that the issue you want to discuss is a highly charged one for that person and could lead to conflict. For example, you may know a person who is usually easy-going. This person has a history of mismanaging money and has become touchy about the issue. If you want to talk about a problem with his or her bookkeeping, you may get a defensive response. On the other hand, there might be someone who usually seems fairly threatening to you, but who is unlikely to get upset about the topic at hand. For example, approaching a "scary" co-worker to ask for money for his or her favorite charity is likely to draw a calm response.

3. How Often Should You Speak Up?

Another way to regulate the amount of risk comes from choosing the *frequency* of risk-taking. When you are starting out, you'll need to go slowly. You may decide to speak up just one out of every ten times, even if you are aware of needs and feelings the other nine times. Later on, as you become more confident, you may move toward speaking up one out of every two or three times.

4. How Intimate Should You Get?

A fourth aspect of calibrating the risk involves deciding the level of intimacy at which you want to talk about the subject. The more you reveal about your feelings and needs and the more you talk about the relationship between you and the other person, the more intimate the conversation becomes. Making a practical, specific request is usually less intimate than talking about how the request fits into the patterns of a relationship. For example, saying to a friend, "How about having dinner together before we go to that movie?" represents less of a risk than, "I've been feeling very close to you recently and I would love to spend more time together. How about having dinner together before that movie?"

Now consider an example of a risk and a fallback position. Perhaps you have a friend who's been calling you, wanting to talk on the telephone more often than you have the time or energy for. You like this friend and you want to maintain the relationship with her, and *My problem!* you also find your enthusiasm for the friendship waning because you've been forcing yourself to talk at times that are inconvenient for you. (Notice the use of "and" in the above dilemma, rather than "but." Some of you may have a tendency to view this sort of dilemma as a set of contradictions, i.e., I like my friend, but I want her to call me more often. The but in that sentence signals that there's an impossible contradiction in the situation.

The and signals that all of your feelings and needs can be addressed.)

If you've been talking to your friend when you haven't felt like it, and if you're fearful of asserting your needs by setting some limits on how often you talk, you may want to begin to set the limits on a very small scale. For example, you might decide that out of the next ten times she calls, you'll say "no" to talking to her one time. Saying no once out of ten times may not solve the problem for you, since perhaps you'd want to say no seven out of ten times. But it begins to give you the experience of saying no and the opportunity to do so in a very low-key way that maximizes your chances of a receptive response. You need the experience of a successful outcome. After a number of successful outcomes, you'll feel ready to proceed in more risky fashions.

You now have five ways of taking care of yourself when you take risks. You have a fallback position for protection when the going gets rough. And you regulate the risk you take by paying attention to whether you're dealing with a high- or low-risk person, what the conflict potential is in the topic, what level of intimacy you're choosing, and how often you choose to talk about a topic.

Being aware of all of these factors lets you determine the level of risk you're prepared to take. You can choose the risk level that's right for you at any given moment. You'll have a sense of control, which will soothe some of the anxiety that naturally accompanies risk-taking.

How To Implement the Program

One powerful way of organizing the process of learning these skills is to keep a journal in which you plan your risk-taking program. You'll want to jot down something about each of your risk-taking experiments–perhaps describing the situation, your feelings and fears about it, your fallback position, and the outcome. While it may seem odd at first to be so planned about your interactions with other people, you'll find that having a clear idea of what you're doing will make your learning go much faster than a trial-and-error approach. The added awareness that you'll bring to your interactions will help you spot where they're going wrong, and find solutions. Eventually, you won't need to be so planned about your contact with others. Like the athlete who has to do everything deliberately at first, with practice you'll use skills spontaneously.

The chart below is an effective way to focus and organize your endeavors. Quantifying the risk will help you measure your progress and ensure that you don't take a larger risk than you're prepared to handle.

Take a look at the chart with a situation in mind in which you might want to speak up about a feeling, express a need, or set a limit. Choose a low-risk situation to start. Let's say you have a roommate with whom you're on good terms with. You find her, in general, an easy person to approach. You've rarely needed to raise any problems with her, but tonight you have a headache and she has her stereo on loud. You would like her to turn it down.

Looking at the chart, think first about how much potential for conflict exists in this situation. Your roommate is pretty easygoing. You assess the issue of her stereo as a minor one, since in the past you've had no objection to her playing it, and therefore she's not likely to get bent out of shape by your request.

Your feeling about your roommate is that she is a low-risk person for you. You find her unintimidating and easy to talk to. In terms of frequency of risk, you haven't raised any issue with her for many months. There's been little stress in your relationship.

As for the intimacy of this particular contact, you don't intend to raise issues involving your entire relationship, nor do you intend to express much feeling. Your request is very circumscribed. It will probably be easy to contain the discussion to a simple, practical level.

On the chart, each low-risk item is given a rating of one, each medium-risk item is rated two, and each high-risk item is rated three. If you mark an "X" in the low-risk column after each item, you come out with a score of four.

Now imagine that you have the same need: you have a headache and your roommate's stereo is painfully loud tonight. In this situation, however, your roommate is someone you find intimidating, and the two of you have not been getting along well at all. You seem to get into squabbles over minor things. You feel she gets angry easily. You've made a number of requests for changes in her behavior over the past few weeks and your hunch is that she'll respond defensively to your request to turn down the stereo. Furthermore, you are upset enough about the situation that you want to initiate a discussion of your relationship, using tonight's stereo problem as a springboard for talking about the troubles that the two of you have been experiencing.

In this case, each of the items in the chart will be marked in the high-risk column. There is a high prob-

LEVEL OF RISK

	HIGH (3)	MEDIUM (2)	LOW (1)
How Risky Is the Topic?			
How Approachable Is This Person?			
How Often Have You Raised Issues?			
How Intimately Do You Want to Talk?			

ability of conflict. Your roommate is a high-risk person to you. There has been a high frequency of risky interactions. And the intimacy level of the conversation will be high since you plan to talk about the foundations of your relationship and whether it is viable. (Intimacy as it is used here is not meant as an equivalent for closeness. An intimate conversation may be a warm and close one, but it may also involve a frank assessment of important aspects of the relationship, or of the foundation of the relationship as a whole.) In this example, the risk score is twelve, which means that the situation represents a very high risk.

This system can help you to assess what you are ready to deal with. For example, if asserting your needs is difficult for you and you haven't had much practice at it, you might feel ready to take on a risk "four," as demonstrated in the first example above. You might know that you're not ready to take on a risk "twelve," as demonstrated in the second example.

You may even decide to let your roommate's stereo continue to bother you on this particular evening. You have a headache and are already feeling out of sorts, so even a risk of four may seem more than you want to deal with. The level of risk you feel ready to take is determined by your strength on a particular day, as well as your general level of risk-taking skills. How often you've tackled a given risk will also influence your decision. You may be at the level of taking a particular risk one in ten times, or you may have graduated to one out of three times.

Consider the fallback positions for these two risks. In the first example, your roommate, although generally receptive and unflappable, may for whatever reason react defensively this time. A fallback position could be: "Regardless of the outcome of this exchange, it's very important for me to speak up about what I need. I'm learning to take care of myself and this is an important part of it. Our friendship is strong enough so that this difference of opinion tonight won't threaten it."

In the second instance, with a risk level of twelve, the greatest risk might be that the two of you will decide that you can't work out your differences and can no longer be roommates. In this case, a fallback position might go something like: "It was really brave of me to go beyond the issue of the stereo to introduce the topic of how frequently we've been clashing. It was necessary to look at our differing needs. Ultimately my needs will be better served by living with someone I get along with. So even though I may be shaken by our talking about not living together, I was fundamentally taking good care of myself by not letting the situation drag on. It was constructive of me to bring up the issue. Now that our problems are out in the open, we have a chance to work on them together."

As you become more and more familiar with this chart, you may find that you are able to apply it at the moment an issue arises without the need to plan it out in advance. Ultimately, the goal of learning these skills is to be able to speak up spontaneously. Eventually, you will intuitively assess the level of risk involved and act in accordance with your level of skill and your readiness to risk at a given moment.

Most people find it an enjoyable process to watch their first shaky baby steps develop into surefooted assertiveness. It's a process that might take you months or even years to master. But the payoff is enormous in terms of freedom of self-expression and ability to get your needs met.

9

Mary: An Example of Risk-Taking

Chapter 8 discussed the need to modulate the risk that you take and suggested a program of graduated risk-taking. Now that you understand what constitutes a risk and how to regulate your risk-taking, it might be useful to follow an imaginary person through a self-regulated program of learning to speak up about needs and feelings. You'll follow Mary as she progresses from small risks to larger and larger ones. You'll look at these risks in the context of her history and her particular strengths and weaknesses.

Mary's Family History

Mary comes from a family in which both her mother and her father exhibited some degree of disturbance. While neither of them was ever diagnosed or treated, Mary and her brothers and sisters knew that something was amiss in their family. As an adult, Mary discovered that a number of her relatives viewed her family as dysfunctional.

Mary's father had a tendency toward violent behavior. As Mary was growing up, she quickly learned that the smallest frustration could send him into a rage; he would throw things and break furniture, and generally intimidate those around him.

Mary's mother was a passive and timid person who showed little emotion. From time to time, she had bouts of serious depression. She would withdraw to her room for several days at a time, becoming unavailable to Mary and her siblings. During these times, Mary's father tended to be particularly volatile. Mary remembers frequently running over to the neighbor's house in fear, looking for protection.

Mary had no model for constructive conflict and healthy assertiveness. Her father expressed frustration through displays of temper; her mother withdrew from conflict situations, taking a passive, resigned stance about her needs.

As an adult, Mary avoids conflict at all costs. It rarely occurs to her to tune in to what she might want or need in a situation, let alone voice such feelings. Because of the amount of intimidation Mary suffered as a child, she brings a lot of fear to her program of learning to speak up. She will need to proceed very slowly. She'll also need compassion for herself, keeping in mind why this learning process will be difficult for her.

Looking at Current Relationships

Mary surveys her life, looking carefully at her work situation, her friendships, and her relationship with her boyfriend. She also examines how she is relating to her parents now that she is an adult. Here is what she finds in each area.

Mary works at a desk in a room shared by several other employees. The woman at the next desk, who she basically likes, smokes a lot of cigarettes. There is no policy where Mary works limiting people's right to smoke. So Mary has been putting up with a great deal of cigarette smoke blowing her way. Fearful of conflict, she hasn't said anything to the woman.

In terms of Mary's friendships, she finds that she has a tendency to become rather isolated. Her pattern seems to be that she will make friends with a person who enjoys what a good listener she is. Before long, that person will begin to turn to Mary with more and more problems. Eventually, Mary begins to feel burdened. She tires of playing counselor and begins to make excuses for not getting together. Over time the relationship atrophies. She eventually makes more friendships based around the same pattern of interacting. Again she eventually withdraws. It is hard for Mary to imagine being in a friendship in which *she* would feel comfortable opening up about her feelings and her needs, where she could turn to a friend for a shoulder to cry on when she feels unhappy.

As for her relationships with men, Mary, who is in her early thirties, went through a long stretch of time in her twenties during which she had one abusive relationship after another. As fearful as she was of her father and as eager as she was to get out of his home, she found herself re-creating that violent relationship via her choice of men.

Following the third such relationship, in which her partner actually became physically violent with her, Mary took a long, hard look at the pattern that was developing. She realized that she had to set out to consciously change this automatic behavior. She made very sure that the next man she chose to be involved with was very different from her father.

Her boyfriend Sam, whom she's been with for two and a half years, is a gentle person. If anything, he tends to be overly quiet about his needs, rarely expressing any frustration or anger. Mary is delighted that she has chosen a partner who doesn't attempt to get his way by intimidating her. She is proud of the progress she's made in freeing herself of abusive relationships. On the other hand, she's quite chagrined to find that frequently when there's something she wants from her boyfriend, she hesitates to speak up for quite some time. She then finds herself exploding into a rage not unlike the ones she witnessed from her father.

Mary is beginning to recognize that she has no models from her childhood for asserting herself in a healthy way. She either does not speak up at all about her needs, like her mother, or she expresses her needs in an abusive fashion, much as her father did. She feels enormously guilty that she is taking advantage of her partner's non-threatening style. Their relationship is satisfying and enjoyable in many ways, and Mary really regrets the stress that her outbursts cause in the relationship.

As for Mary's current relationship with her mother and father, there are some serious problems here, too. Mary's father has become more disturbed over the years and his outbursts more frequent. Furthermore, even when he is not in a rage, his general stance toward the people around him and the world at large seems to be increasingly paranoid. He trusts no one and seems to assume that everyone is out to get him.

Mary's mother, meanwhile, has begun to turn to Mary, the oldest of the siblings, for comfort and advice in dealing with her father. Mary gets frequent phone calls, sometimes very late at night, from her mother. Mary also suspects her mother is starting to drink too much, judging by her sometimes incoherent and slurred speech.

Mary has moved many thousands of miles away from her home in order to leave her dysfunctional family behind. Yet in recent years she finds herself becoming more and more embroiled with their problems. She's also realizing, as her mother asks for more and more help from her, that this pattern of seeking advice and help began when Mary was a child. It was somewhat more subtle and less urgent, but the message was there—Mary had to soothe her mother, rather than vice versa. Mary is increasingly aware that she needs to set some limits on her mother's requests for help and support. As for her father, her annual visits to her family have become uncomfortable enough so that she's considering stopping the visits altogether in order to avoid dealing with him face-to-face. So far, however, Mary hasn't taken any steps toward remedying her dilemma with her family.

Recognizing a Pattern

As Mary takes stock of her life, she begins to see a clear theme running throughout the different areas and relationships in her life. She notices it's very difficult for her to be forthcoming about her feelings and needs and to do so in a constructive manner. Mary has some potentially very satisfying aspects to her life. If she can learn the tools for healthy assertion, there's no reason why she can't have a great deal of pleasure and intimacy in her relationships. The key here is for Mary to take this one step at a time, and to maximize the success of each step by taking on only what she is prepared to handle at any given time.

Deciding Where to Start

In thinking this over, Mary realizes that her cigarette smoking colleague at work might be the best problem to tackle first since it's a daily aggravation. However, she carefully assesses the risk factors involved, not allowing the sense of urgency to cloud her judgment about what level of risk she is ready to handle. She considers the nature of her relationship with the woman at the next desk, and assesses her basic temperament. The two of them have been getting along very well since the new woman joined the office. She notes that the woman, whose name is Helen, seems to be easygoing, friendly, and in general quite considerate. So Helen seems to Mary to be a non-threatening sort of person, one she would place in the low-risk category. Furthermore, Mary usually has an easier time bringing up issues with women than with men, given her history with her violent father.

As for the frequency of risk, Mary isn't feeling overdosed on risk-taking. In fact, she's ready to begin to take on more than she has previously. In terms of her relationship with Helen, they haven't had to work out anything between them yet, so their relationship is far from overloaded with conflict.

As for the intimacy involved in this risk, Mary's intention is to talk very little about her feelings or their relationship as a whole, and to focus strictly on the specific issue of smoking. Therefore, the risk on an intimacy level is quite low.

In terms of the conflict potential of the issue–talking about Helen's smoking–Mary senses that this may involve slightly more risk. She can imagine that smoking may be a sore subject for Helen. Clearly, this is an area where Mary's needs and Helen's needs are in direct opposition.

So, in rating the risk factors involved in talking to Helen, Mary rates all of the risks at one except the area of conflict potential, to which she assigns a three. This gives her a score of six for this particular risk. A score of four would be the lowest risk that she could take, and normally it might be advisable to begin risk-taking around a score of four or five. In this case, Mary decides that she's feeling enough urgency about the situation and sturdy enough about beginning to take some risks that she will tackle this risk with a rating of six.

Here's how the conversation between Mary and Helen goes:

Mary: Helen, I'd like to talk to you about a problem I'm having with your smoking. Smoke drifts over to my desk and bothers me. Could we spend a few minutes figuring out how to change this?

Helen: Oh! I didn't realize that my smoking was bothering you. Sure, let's see what we can come up with. Have you thought about what you'd like me to do?

Mary: Would you be willing to smoke out in the hallway?

Helen: Well, sometimes that would be okay, but sometimes I need to smoke when I'm feeling particularly pressured by a deadline and there's really no time to take a break. Do you think it would help if we put up a fan blowing away from your desk?

Mary: Yeah, that sounds like a great idea! I could buy us one today on my lunch hour. Gee, that's a relief. I was pretty nervous about bringing this up with you.

Helen: Really? How come?

Mary: Well, it's not easy for me to make requests–it's something I'm just learning to do and I didn't know whether or not smoking is a touchy issue for you like it is for some people.

Helen: Well actually, it is kind of a loaded subject for me. I've tried to quit a number of times and feel like kind of a failure for not succeeding. But you didn't seem to be judging me when you brought it up so I didn't feel too defensive. But what did you mean about just learning to make requests?

Mary: Oh, I'm actually making a project of learning to speak up about my needs and at this point I still get scared every time I do it.

Taking on More Risks

Heartened by the positive outcome of this particular risk, Mary is encouraged to take similar circumscribed risks with other colleagues around more minor annoyances. For example, one colleague habitually takes Mary's assigned parking place. Another is chronically late in giving Mary certain written reports, which then forces Mary to be late in turning in her share of the work. Most of these risks are in the five to six range for Mary, and she practices at taking one of these approximately once a week.

In some instances, Mary runs into less than favorable responses to her requests. Here we have an example. Mary approaches Bruce, the colleague whose car blocks her parking spot.

Mary: I often find your car in my parking spot when I arrive in the morning and I end up driving around looking for a spot on the street. I'd like it if you'd stop taking my place.

Bruce: Well, I don't think it's fair that you have an assigned spot while I don't. I have to look for parking on the street most of the time. Besides, you're only here four days a week and I'm here five.

Mary is taken aback and quickly drops the conversation. Thinking it over later, she realizes that she felt guilty when Bruce complained that she had an assigned spot while he didn't. She was then further confused by his statement about her only being in the office four days while he was there five. She reminds herself that she has a right to make requests and to set limits when she feels encroached upon. She also recognizes that Bruce's response was an indirect way of telling her that she didn't have a right to what she wanted. She returns to the conversation with him.

Mary: Bruce, about the parking space we were talking about the other day. I can understand that you resent my having an assigned spot here when you don't, but the system here at the company, as you probably know, is that people who have worked here the longest have the assigned spots. Whenever a place becomes available, the next person in line gets it. I'm sorry that there aren't enough spots to go around, but that's not my responsibility. I've worked here longer than you have, and that's how I got my spot. It's fine with me if you'd like to use my spot on the days when I'm not here in the office, but I would like it to be kept free for me on the four days that I am here.

Bruce: I don't think the policy is very fair. I think we should draw lots to see who gets spaces.

Mary: Well, if you want to initiate something like that, that's up to you. But in the meantime, it's my spot and I'd like you to leave it free for me.

In this dialogue, Mary is able to hold fast to her position and not assume responsibility for the office parking problems. She offers what she can, the use of her spot on the days when she isn't in the office, and insists on her right to her spot the rest of the time. Mary leaves the second conversation feeling good about having held her ground, but also a little shaky about the confrontation. She again reminds herself of her right to assert her needs. When she arrives at work the next day and finds her parking spot available, she is very pleased with herself for having stood up for her right to her spot. She finds that even though Bruce didn't do a good job of communicating with her around this issue, he now leaves her spot vacant. Furthermore, she notes that the sense of tension between them eases over time.

Moving on to Larger Risks

After a few weeks of mostly successful outcomes and of handling well those instances where her requests are met with less than favorable responses, Mary feels ready to tackle a slightly more intimate situation. She decides to attempt to change her pattern of being the good listener who doesn't ask for attention. This issue is an important one for her. It also seems somewhat less scary than tackling her relationship with her boyfriend or her parents. She scans her friendships and does some initial rating of the risk potential involved in each. She evaluates how risky the topic is, how comfortable she feels with the other person, how often she has raised issues with that person, and at what level of intimacy she wants to approach the person.

Mary starts with her friend Kenneth. She assesses the conflict potential in the situation to be rather low. She feels that her desire to move beyond the good listener role in their relationship is likely to be welcomed by Kenneth. She is basing this assessment on the fact that he has occasionally commented on how little she talks about herself, and has indicated a desire to hear more about her life and her concerns. Furthermore, there has been no history of friction between them.

In the case of her friendship with Roberta, however, Mary's assessment of the situation is quite different. Roberta is an intense and sometimes volatile person with whom Mary, in spite of her tendency to avoid conflict, has had occasional skirmishes, including a recent one. Furthermore, Roberta, who has been going through a messy breakup of a relationship, just last week complained to Mary that some of their mutual friends seemed to be losing interest in hearing about the breakup. Roberta felt that her friends' attention was limited when she was feeling especially needy. It's clear to Mary, in sizing up her relationship with Roberta, that tackling this dynamic between them at this time represents a very high risk.

Using the same format, Mary evaluates each of her relationships. She ranks them in terms of the risk involved in tackling her problem of always being the listener. She then decides the frequency with which she'll address this issue in each relationship. For example, for Kenneth, with whom she anticipates pretty smooth sailing, she assigns herself the task of addressing the issue one out of three times that it occurs. With Roberta, on the other hand, she'll raise the issue one out of ten times. Furthermore, with Kenneth she'll address the issue in a more intimate fashion than she will with Roberta. For example, with Kenneth she'll talk about the pattern of listening rather than talking to him about herself. She'll let him know she's tackling this pattern within their relationship and in her other relationships. She will also enlist his support in noticing when this starts to happen between them. With Roberta, on the other hand, Mary decides that she will not discuss the issue, but will simply, one time out of ten, make a strong attempt to turn the conversation in the direction of discussing her own concerns.

There are other friends and acquaintances who fall in a more intermediate area for Mary. With them she might risk one time out of five, talking about the issue with various degrees of intimacy.

Mary now has a game plan for tackling the problem of not asking for attention from her friends. She considers the positive nature of this project and accordingly prepares herself a fallback position. She wants one that supports and encourages her growth in this area regardless of the particular outcome of any one interaction. She writes: "It's important that I'm learning to ask for attention and support in my relationships. Regardless of whether a particular friend is receptive or not, my willingness to open up about my needs is important progress." She is now ready to begin what will probably be several months worth of work in her friendships in this particular area.

Signs of Progress

Within a few months, Mary has accomplished a great deal in changing her habit of listening to her friends and not talking about her own concerns. Many of her friendships are now more balanced. She continues to provide her friends with a warm and interested ear, but now she also opens up more often about whatever is on her mind. She has found most of her friends to be receptive and, in fact, appreciative of her increased sharing.

Sure enough, her first attempt to bring up the problem with Kenneth was a success. He was delighted to hear that she'd recognized the problem herself. He told her that he's become curious to hear more about her, but hadn't wanted to intrude. He was also beginning to feel awkward about always being the one to talk in their conversations. That first conversation centered around Mary describing her difficulty in opening up. Although it was hard conveying to Kenneth exactly why she felt so nervous, it was clear he wanted to listen and understand. After the conversation, Mary felt both pleased with herself and closer to Kenneth.

Unfortunately, but predictably, the first attempt to say something to Roberta was less successful. Encouraged by her talk with Kenneth, Mary had decided to talk to Roberta the very next time she called. Roberta was particularly upset that evening and called Mary in tears. Although Mary later decided she should have waited, she told Roberta she was in the middle of something and had to hang up. Roberta answered angrily, "Thanks–some help you are. I guess *no one* cares how I'm feeling." She hung up before Mary even had a chance to respond. Mary was about to call back and apologize but instead she went to her journal and reread her fallback statement. She also read the positive things she had written after her talk with Kenneth. In a little while, Roberta herself called back to apologize, acknowledging that Mary really did listen and respond to her almost all of the time. "I guess I didn't realize how demanding I can get," she said. Roberta did continue to call every few days, but Mary knew Roberta would be more understanding the next time Mary introduced her own needs or limits.

In the process of tackling the issue of asking for attention in her friendships, a number of things have emerged for Mary. She's found that she frequently has to challenge a strong feeling that her friends will not be interested in hearing what she has to say. She has done some work on tracing these feelings back to her deprived childhood, challenging the accuracy of these feelings in her present relationships. Almost every time Mary has pushed past her assumption that a particular friend will not be interested in what she has to say, her friend's response has helped to dispel this ingrained notion a little more.

Furthermore, Mary is finding that many of her relationships are becoming closer and richer, a result of a more balanced and lively give and take. In those instances where Mary has chosen to share with a friend the work that she is doing about this issue, she has carved new territory for the two of them. They have discussed the changes that they would like to make in their relationships.

Mary has also learned more about her friends. There are some friends with whom Mary's slightest efforts to make more room for herself in the relationships are effective. These friends seem immediately to sense Mary's desire to take the floor, and welcome it.

With other friends, she has to push a little harder to get that kind of room for herself. In one friendship, Mary has found that no matter how hard she asserts herself about taking time for herself, her friend shows little interest in what Mary has to say, and turns the conversation back to herself as quickly as possible. After repeated attempts in this particular relationship, Mary is beginning to realize that this friend holds little genuine interest in Mary. Mary is considering backing off from that friendship.

Mary is also finding that she has an increasingly good feeling about herself. This comes from the mostly positive experiences of asking for more of what she needs and from changing the nature of her friendships. This increased self-confidence helps her to feel ready to tackle some of the most intimate relationships in her life–namely, those with her boyfriend and with her parents.

Confronting the Family

Mary's mother has been turning to her more and more often for help. Her mother's phone calls have increased during the past months, as Mary has been tackling these issues in her friendships. Mary decides that setting some limits with her mother about the phone calls is becoming increasingly necessary. She considers how to approach the problem. For example, she could broach the issue in terms of the overall dynamics of their relationship, expressing her feelings about how much her mother has always leaned on her. Or she could approach the issue in a much more limited fashion, simply saying, "I'm not free to talk right now," and then get off the phone.

Mary decides that there is little chance that her mother will be open to exploring and possibly changing the dynamics of their relationship. The stress that her mother is experiencing with her husband as well as her increasing use of alcohol seem to leave her little emotional room for developing a healthier relationship with her daughter.

Mary sets herself an initial goal of saying "no" to her mother one time out of five. She plans to increase this to one time out of three after the first two weeks. Mary anticipates quite a bit of protest from her mother. When Mary prepares her fallback position, she is careful to define the experiment as a success regardless of her mother's responses.

As Mary begins to tackle this issue, she discovers a lot of variation in how much her mother accepts or fights Mary's attempts to get off the phone. Mary carefully monitors her tendency to give in if her mother attempts to keep her on the phone. She notes the feelings of guilt and obligation that quickly arise, and uses her fallback position to assure herself that what she is doing is positive and necessary.

After Mary's mother has called her several nights in a row, Mary decides it's time to say no to her.

Mother: I'm having a hard night. Your dad was so difficult today, and now I can't fall asleep.

Mary: I'm sorry you're awake so late, but I was just falling asleep and I want to go back to bed. How about if we talk another time?

Mother: But I'm afraid I'll be up all night.

Mary: I hope you won't, but at any rate I need to get *my* sleep. Let's talk another time. Goodnight.

Mary feels quite guilty as she hangs up. She immediately reads her fallback position. It reassures her that setting limits on her mother's constant calling is healthy and necessary for Mary and for their relationship. She remembers that if she doesn't do this, she'll feel increasingly resentful. If she does set limits, she'll have a better chance of being wholeheartedly interested and supportive when they *do* talk.

At the end of four weeks, Mary is ready to tell her mother "no" each time the call is inconvenient. Since the calls frequently come at an inconvenient time, Mary decides that it would be helpful to discuss openly with her mother the change that is occurring in the pattern of their relationship. She chooses to do this because she speculates that her mother must be noticing the change in her behavior. Mary feels that acknowledging and clarifying what she is doing would be useful. The conversation goes like this:

Mary: Mom, I've been wanting to talk to you about something. Have you noticed that when you call, some of the time I've been saying I can't talk to you?

Mother: Yes, of course. In fact, I figured you must be angry with me about something.

Mary: No, I'm not angry with you. But you've been calling an awful lot recently. For a while I felt like I should talk to you each time. I realized that I really need to say no to you when it's not a good time to talk. I hope that doesn't hurt your feelings.

Mother: I knew you were probably getting tired of me. Everybody seems to eventually. But I was hoping that because you were my daughter *you'd* hang in with me. After all, I've always been there for *you* when you needed something. Things are pretty hard these days and I don't seem to have a lot of friends right now. It's pretty cold of you to turn me away.

Mary: Mom, I *am* hanging in with you. That's why I'm talking to you about this. I'd like to work things out so that I can give you the support that you need while taking care of my own needs at the same time. I think that's possible. I know you're going through a hard time. Sometimes when you call me it's not a good time for me to talk, and I'd rather talk to you when I can give you my wholehearted attention.

Mother: That makes sense. I got nervous that you were saying you didn't want to talk with me anymore. So many of my friends seem to have burned out on my problems that I was afraid you were going to stop wanting to talk to me too. I know I've been calling a lot, and I do feel kind of bad that I'm burdening you with all my problems.

Mary: Mom, you're not burdening me as long as I don't talk to you at times that are really inconvenient for me. I worry about you, especially with Dad seeming like he's in worse and worse shape. I know you're having a hard time. In fact, maybe this is none of my business, but sometimes on the phone, you seem like you've been drinking.

Mother: Well, maybe sometimes I have a drink or two to calm my nerves, but I don't think it's anything to worry about. You'd probably want a drink or two if you were in my situation.

Mary: Well, this may not be the right time to talk about it, but let's talk about it some more sometime soon, because I am concerned about it.

Mother: There's really nothing to talk about.

In this conversation Mary refuses to be sidetracked by her mother's guilt-inducing statements and continues to reassert her needs and limits. Her mother eventually comes around to accepting the limits and seeing that Mary is not rejecting her. Mary then introduces the subject of her mother's drinking. Given immediate denial on her mother's part, she decides to simply reassert that she believes it's an issue, and table the discussion for another time.

In the context of this increased communication between Mary and her mother, Mary finds it relatively easy at one point to let her mother know how uncomfortable she feels these days with her father's increasing paranoia. She shares with her mother that she has been seriously considering not coming for a visit this year. The two of them are able to talk about ways that Mary might visit, with a minimal amount of contact with her father.

Confronting Her Boyfriend

Heartened by her improvement in dealing with her family situation, Mary now turns her attention to her relationship with her boyfriend. She notices that during the months she's been practicing speaking up about her needs at work and with her friends and her mother, there have been fewer incidents of becoming emotionally abusive with her boyfriend. In fact, she's found it easier to speak up sooner rather than later about her feelings and needs. Therefore her feelings haven't built up as frequently to the point where she is angry. However, she feels that this area of her life still needs some attention, since at times it's still difficult for her to express herself to her boyfriend.

She rates the risks involved in this enterprise. She feels that Sam, her boyfriend, is a very non-threatening person, relaxed and easy to talk with. When she's able to speak up about her needs, he generally seems quite receptive. On the other hand, some of the issues she still shies away from do have a pretty high potential for conflict. As for the level of intimacy, these particular issues need to be dealt with in terms of the overall dynamics of their relationship. Therefore the discussion must be a broad one, not simply limited to behavioral changes.

For example, it seems that in one way or another Mary has been ending up doing most of the household chores and the cooking, whereas the two of them agreed long ago that housework should be divided evenly between them. This stereotyped sex-role division of labor has been creeping into their relationship more and more. Mary recognizes that at times there have been extenuating circumstances–Sam took on a new job, for instance, which has kept him busy and exhausted. However, she's noticed that even when his work load eases up, she's still doing most of the housework. Up to now she has been handling this by passively continuing to do more than her share. Occasionally she has found herself blowing up about minor, and unavoidable, annoyances.

The other area that Mary wants to talk to Sam about seems riskier to her. She's been feeling some strain in their sex life because more and more she has become the main initiator of sexual contact between them. Mary has been telling herself that perhaps this pattern between them has to do with the fact that Sam has been overworked in his new job, feeling tired and unenthusiastic about making love. Still, Mary finds herself becoming increasingly insecure. She notices that she is beginning to retreat from any impulse to reach out to him. She doesn't want to let her tendency to withdraw go unchecked.

Mary prepares a fallback position to use with each of these risks. The fallback position addresses the importance of moving forward in her relationship with Sam and of not allowing negative feelings to build up. She defines her willingness to bring up these matters as positive regardless of how any one exchange between them turns out. In the long run, she knows she is improving the health of their relationship.

Mary: Sam, let's talk about how we're handling the household chores. I think that I've been doing most of the cooking and cleaning for some time now. I'd like us to share the work more equally.

Sam: Yeah, you're right about that. But I've noticed that I seem to be doing the lion's share of the maintenance around the house. I've actually been feeling a little resentful about that and I figured that letting you do more of the cleaning kind of makes us more even.

Mary: Gee, I didn't know that was going on. Now that I think about it, I guess you have been spending a lot of time repairing things. You know, I'm not crazy about the way this is sliding into a typical sex role division of labor. Let's talk about whether we really want to divide up the chores this way.

This leads to a long and frank discussion of the ways in which they inadvertently slip into sex-role division of labor. They talk about which aspects of this division are acceptable and unacceptable to each of them. They also use the opportunity to examine whether there are other areas of their relationship where they are following stereotyped behaviors.

Mary tackles the sexual issue next. She finds this one a hard issue to broach. She has to do some internal work on her tendency to assume that she is accurate in her feeling that Sam is rejecting her. She manages to approach him with some open-mindedness and curiosity about what is actually going on with him.

Mary: Sam, I've been feeling somewhat concerned about our sex life. It seems like I've been doing most of the initiating for quite some time and it's getting harder for me to keep reaching out. For a while, I thought maybe it was your new job, feeling overworked and tired and all, but over the last few weeks I've been feeling more and more insecure. Is there something going wrong between us?

Sam: Nothing's the matter–I've just been tired sometimes. Besides, I don't think you've been doing all the initiating. Let's not make a big deal out of this.

Mary: Well, our sex life is important to me and I don't want to start feeling insecure. Since I've been worrying about the change I see, I really do feel a need for us to talk about it. How about if you take a little time to think about whether there's anything else going on and then we could talk about it again in a few days.

This is new behavior for Mary, feeling free to pursue the topic even though she wasn't initially met with a positive response. When the two of them return to the discussion a few days later, Mary finds that Sam has given a lot of thought to the issue.

Sam: I've been thinking about what you brought up the other day and I'm sorry that you've been feeling shut out. Now I realize there's more going on than just tiredness from the new job, but it doesn't have to do with my feelings for *you*. What's really going on is that I've been feeling lousy about *myself*. I feel like I'm not doing very well at the new job, and I can't seem to quit putting myself down. I keep comparing myself with the guy who had the job before me; he was much better at it. When I feel bad about myself, it's hard for me to imagine that you can still find me attractive. It's been hard for me to take a chance on reaching out to you.

As Sam opens up about the pain he's been in, Mary is relieved to hear that his behavior hasn't been a reflection of unloving feelings toward her. She feels compassion for the difficult time he's going through. This exchange brings them closer than they've been for many months, and lays the groundwork for a freer sharing of a variety of feelings between them.

Mary reviews what she has accomplished over the past six months in learning to express her feelings and her needs. She finds that although it's an ongoing process of practicing and learning in all the areas of her life, she has achieved the goals she initially set. She also finds that as she feels more and more sturdy about expressing herself, her relationships grow richer. This encourages even more self-expression within those relationships. There's a positive snowballing effect happening for her.

Hints for Hanging in

Mary's experiences have been described in somewhat oversimplified terms for the sake of this example. Most of you will encounter more twists and turns in the road than Mary did. You may need to ask yourself at certain points why you're afraid to take the next risk, or why a given exchange turned out in an unconstructive fashion. However, if you keep the overall goals in mind, these temporary setbacks will simply be part of practicing a new skill, like the skier who accepts that falling down is part of learning to ski.

If you do find yourself repeatedly struggling in certain ways, you may want to get some help. Close friends, for instance, can often be helpful in giving you feedback on ways that you may be inadvertently sabotaging yourself or getting caught up in fears that are disproportionate to the risk involved.

It's important to keep in mind that you need to approach this project with a lot of patience. It's not easy making up for the support and comfort you missed as a child. But if you give yourself plenty of time and plenty of soothing, you will find that you can indeed develop the skills you didn't learn in your family.

Previous chapters have examined the childhood origins of many of the difficulties you may be having in your adult life–problems in your self-esteem, problems in relationships, problems in your work world. They've also discussed a number of avenues for approaching these issues. These pathways to change have fallen mainly into two categories. The first involves increasing your self-knowledge by understanding the historical origins of your difficulties. The second is based on learning to observe carefully your current feelings and behavior, experimenting with changes in self-expression. Awareness of what you're experiencing in a moment-to-moment sense allows you to begin to make different choices about your behavior. You're working with both your internal emotions and your external actions.

When viewed in this manner, the large, amorphous, and sometimes overwhelming goal of "wanting to change" can be broken down into little steps involving small but important risks. Many of you will find that approaching the idea of changing your life in a structured and methodical manner is reassuring and manageable. But what's implied in this approach is the willingness to practice. Just as the artist or musician must focus his time and awareness on his art, learning all the skills associated with it, the person who wishes to learn about his or her patterns, reclaim buried emotions, and develop new behavioral habits must approach this goal in a patient and disciplined fashion.

Change is generally very slow. All of us would love to be able to make the desired changes in our lives rapidly and easily. However, the vast majority of ACMIs find that while there are often spurts of rapid growth, in general change is a slow, evolving process, measured in months and years rather than in minutes and weeks. It's important to know and accept this fact if you are to undertake a major reclamation project. In order to recover some of the buried parts of yourself and make room for previously untapped abilities to flourish, you'll need to respect your own rhythms and your own pace.

There are some ways you can encourage yourself to keep your spirits up even during those times when progress is slow. Many ACMIs find that outside support is useful during this time. This support may involve sharing with friends the discoveries you are making or the frustrations you are facing. For many of you, the help of an ACMI support group, or the assistance of an individual therapist who understands these issues, can be useful in keeping you on track and offering encouragement. Furthermore, a group can allow you to witness and participate in other people's struggles and growth, and thereby help you to understand your own better.

If a therapy group or individual therapy isn't an option, you can still seek out new models. By realizing that you need some of the input that you missed as a child, you can begin to observe how other people handle situations that are difficult for you. For instance, if you have trouble setting limits or asking for what you need, you can watch people at work or in social organizations, or observe your friends who are good at those things.

Another useful technique that can give you a sense of continuity and a way to measure progress is to keep a journal. The journal might include the feelings and memories you get in touch with as you begin to explore your past. Your journal may also include some of the experiences and emotions that emerge as you begin to experiment with new behaviors. A journal can be a good friend to talk to when you're feeling confused and need to think things through, or when you're feeling despondent and need to pour out some feelings in the safety of your own room.

Whichever techniques you employ, whatever pathways work for you, it is important to always remember that you're not the only one struggling with these issues. Because there are many millions of people suffering from mental illness, there are millions of other ACMIs struggling with problems similar to yours. The real miracle is that all of you are survivors. The fact that you're able and willing to pick up this book is an indication that you've survived your childhood and arrived in adulthood, perhaps in some pain or difficulty, but intact enough to want more self-knowledge. Having survived means that you've acquired more strength and skill than you may be aware of. As you tackle some of the ways in which you're dissatisfied with your life, it may help to keep in mind that you probably bring to that endeavor a great deal of both endurance and sensitivity. As you acquire a deeper understanding of why you may be having problems and as you receive some guidelines for how to begin to deal with those issues, a great deal of progress and fulfillment is possible for you.

Part III

Along the Road
to Recovery

"I still find it so amazing that somebody else went through the same stuff I did. And it's also amazing how they have the same problems that I have; it's just unbelievable. Just hearing from other people has been a big help."

–an ACMI

10

Messages of Hope: ACMIs Talk to Each Other

In their interviews, a number of ACMIs spoke about the guidance they'd longed for when first beginning to face their painful histories. They shared with me some thoughts they'd like to communicate to other ACMIs trying to recover from a difficult past. They spoke about many different aspects of their lives, thinking about times that had been especially hard, imagining what would have been helpful to hear at those moments. Here are some of their thoughts:

- About not living in a normal family:

  "You should know that yours is not the only strange family in existence. A lot of my information about other families was from television. So I thought everyone was the 'Leave It to Beaver' family. That really made me depressed."

- About learning to trust:

  "There *are* people who are trustworthy. The whole world is not untrustworthy. There is kindness, and it's genuine, it's believable. For so long I couldn't believe that *anybody* was genuine at all. And it's a real surprise to discover that people really are."

- About finding your way out of a corner:

"You just latch onto anybody who's offering help out of a bad situation and into something that feels softer or kinder. You just follow your nose—even if your nose only goes one little step, you go one step. The picture will look a little bigger. And then you can see a little bit more. And then you can follow your step one more baby step. You just keep doing it until the picture just gets bigger and bigger."

- About feeling child-like:

"Trust being young. It's all right to be young. There are a lot of people who won't shame you for being emotionally young."

- About the hard work of recovery:

"It will have its ups and downs. But probably, if you persist at it, you will come out on the other end. It seems sometimes that you're taking two steps forward and then one step backward. But even at that pace you're still going to make progress.

Just know that it won't be real easy sometimes. Really looking at areas of your life can be very painful. Sometimes it's easier not to look at it, just to feel numb rather than to feel the pain. But by feeling the pain, you get the joy later on that you never will get if you don't go through the pain.

It's still hard for me to do that. You know, to face an issue that I know will be difficult. And even though intellectually I *know* I'll come out of it and feel a lot better, sometimes it's still hard for me to go through the work of it. But I know enough now that I'm pretty good about eventually pushing myself to do it. You do have to push. You have to be real motivated, because nobody can do it except you. But it's worth it."

- Breaking out of survivor's guilt:

"Try very, very hard to have as normal a life as possible and let yourself enjoy it. I think that's maybe the most important thing. It's tough enough having that impairment situation with the parent being mentally ill. It doesn't mean that you shouldn't have a life."

*

"Even if you love your parents, do only what you can for them. I'm not advocating *not* doing things for them. Just don't do too much at your expense, because when they go, you're all you've got. You deserve to have a better life than that mentally disturbed parent had."

- About trying to run away from the past:

"I guess in my own life I have found there is no way I can get away from my past, try as I have. I've had to deal with it, rather than run away from it. I would say, 'Forget running away. You're just not going to make it. And in whatever way you do it, go ahead and deal with it.' You know, I do feel like I've come out the other end of it, and I think others can make it too."

- About coming to terms with your disturbed parent:

"Well, first you have to free yourself from a certain amount of your own internal stuff before you can see what that parent is like in a more rational way. You have to take care of yourself. And in getting help for yourself, you can get a better picture of what they're really like, and how they got that way.

When you're getting help, you don't have to be so understanding of your parents. You have to get your feelings out. And depending on how they are and how they treat you, you may never want to see them again. If there's a chance that you can really communicate, it's a wonderful thing. If you can reach some kind of closeness and communication with your parents, that's wonderful. If you can't, then say goodbye if you have to. Just take care of yourself; do what you have to do."

• Getting help in recovery:

"For me one of the things that helped me in my recovery was not having my story be secret any more, and having some places to talk about it—you know, I started out in therapy talking about it, which was a pretty safe place. But I also talked about it with friends and people in my life. That was very healing also, to not have to hide or pretend it hadn't happened.

The other thing is for people to really try to have their own support in their life. Whatever state your parent's in—whether the person is still really mentally ill or recovered—in either case you really need a place for *you*. You need people that you can talk to and places where you can cry and get mad. And much of that really needs to be separate from the parent, especially if the person is still really disturbed, you don't have much chance to work it out with them. Try to remember that you have a right to live your life no matter what. And try to find things that give you joy and go for it, and do them."

*

"I feel that other people might have other things that work for them, but because I'm an artist, I've done a lot of it through some kind of self-expression. I've done a bunch of writing. I've written a short story about some of my childhood. And I actually did a radio program with my mother. I've done some theater about it. So I think if you can, find a place to express it in whatever way works for you. That changed it for me."

11

For the Helping Professional: Working With the ACMI

Many therapists, in stopping to think about it, find they have certain preconceptions about ACMIs. A typical viewpoint was expressed by one therapist:

> "Sometimes I'll be working with someone who seems fairly stable. When I find out that one of their parents sounds pretty disturbed, or was institutionalized, I'm surprised that they're as together as they are. So I must have an unconscious assumption that disturbed people will have disturbed children."

I asked ACMIs what they would want a therapist to understand about people with their backgrounds. One young woman spoke about growing up with a manic-depressive mother, and the pain of feeling different. She expressed her mixed feelings about how she wants to be seen:

> "Treat us normally. We want so badly just to be normal like everybody else. On the other hand,

we're not *quite* the same. It's very difficult to be 'the same' given what we grew up with... I think maybe we're more fragile than a lot of other kinds of people. We've been disappointed a lot in life. I think we have more fear of dealing with difficult things because we've seen someone who can't. Encourage us that we can do things, and that we can love and be loved, because we can. But understand that some things are more scary for us, and it might take a little more for us to overcome things."

The ACMI typically suffers problems in mastering early developmental tasks. As with any individual from a dysfunctional family, the severity of the disturbance depends on many factors, such as how old the child was when the parent first showed signs of serious mental illness, which parent of the two was disturbed, and what role the emotionally healthier parent assumed in the family. Also, other family members are particularly important since frequently an older sibling offers some substitute parenting. And, of course, the family's support system in terms of extended family and community plays a role in the amount of support the family in crisis received. However, in almost all cases, the loss of a parent to emotional illness leads to a sense of abandonment and to a premature pressure to assume grown-up physical and emotional tasks.

Furthermore, because of the ACMI's experience with an unpredictable parental environment, issues of control tend to be of paramount importance. The ACMI often has wrested control out of the chaos of his home environment at a high price. Many of these individuals hold themselves together with an inordinate need for structure and predictability.

Not surprising, the ACMI's trust both in himself (in his internal world) and in others is usually quite low. While many ACMIs are able to get along socially—indeed many present a very well developed social image—in working with the ACMI one rapidly finds a core of fear and distrust. The degree of this distrust will vary with the kinds of experiences that the ACMI had with the healthier parent and with the other members of his family. However, the severe disturbance of one of the parents with the attendant lack of dependability has in almost all cases left some scars.

Like most individuals from dysfunctional families, ACMIs usually suffer from low self-esteem. They need help in getting past the belief that their disappointing family life was a punishment for some basic inadequacy of the self. This inadequacy is often experienced in terms of guilt over not having been able to love and repair the injured parent, as well as shame about the stigmatization of the family. Often there is also buried rage that many ACMIs feel toward their disturbed parent, which is a source of tremendous guilt.

The treatment of the ACMI, therefore, needs to unfold slowly and gently, with a sensitivity at each point to what your client is ready to handle. Consistency and predictability in the therapy setting is extremely important when dealing with these early issues. The client may do a fair amount of testing to determine whether you, as the helper, are more dependable than their disturbed parent. On the other hand, because there's often a deep loneliness within many of these clients, who frequently grew up feeling isolated from "normal" families and activities, the ACMI is often very hungry to be seen and understood. If approached empathically, they will often learn to open up about their pain and to develop a healthy ability to relate.

While it is, of course, impossible to generalize about this entire population, I have been struck by how, as a survivor of a very difficult childhood, the ACMI has certain traits that foster progress in therapy. The ACMI frequently will be willing to endure a lot of discomfort for the sake of increased self-knowledge and growth. Those ACMIs who have managed to survive their chaotic childhoods have good reality testing and extremely sensitive emotional antennae. While they often use their perceptiveness to anticipate danger in their environment, they can learn to use this gift to further their interpersonal contact, rather than use it for defensive purposes. Furthermore, because many ACMIs grew up with much silence and denial in their families about the dysfunctional parent, they often have a strong hunger for the truth. This dislike of artifice tends to make them honest about themselves and what they see around them. At times they may hold back from naming what they see from fear of retaliation, but once they find the safety to give voice to their perceptions, their vision and honesty tend to be quite acute.

Because of the extreme isolation of growing up in a family within a culture that stigmatizes mental illness, this particular population is especially in need of the sharing and support that a group setting offers. I have found time and again in my groups that, totally apart from any specific therapeutic interventions, the simple experience of being in a room with others who share a similar background is a tremendously healing experience. They're able to talk freely about the sense of shame with which many of them grew up, as well as the ostracism many them faced with their peers.